HARSH TREATMENT

Hammond, J.

COPY 2

LINKS 33

First published in 1988.
Links are published quarterly by Third World First,
232 Cowley Rd, Oxford OX4 1UH

Editors: Jenny Hammond, Luis Reveco
Series editor: Jenny Hammond
We gratefully acknowledge the contributions and editorial assistance of Louise Garner, Michelle
Reeves, Chris Taylor

Links: One year's subscription £10 for individuals, £15 for organisations,
(plus £2.50 a year for surface mail overseas and £6.50 for airmail).
Previous publications are available - please send for details.

Third World First is a development group which has grown out of the efforts of students in
higher education to understand the issues of international poverty and to combat it through
campaigning. Local groups are active at colleges and universities throughout Britain. The
national organisation produces a wide range of publications and runs conferences and campaigns. For more information and details of how to join, contact one of our three offices.

232 Cowley Rd, Oxford OX4 1UH
(0865-245678)

9 Poland St,London W1V 3DG
(01-434 4220)

109 Pilgrim St
Newcastle NE1 6QS
(091-222 0290)

Design layout Petra Pryke (01-243 1464)
Typeset by Phil Armstrong (0865-250922)
Printed by DOT Press (0865-727207)
Trade distribution by TWP (021-773 6572)

ISSN 0261 4014   **ISBN 1 870169 01 8**

CONTENTS

About the Contributors

Yasmin Alibhai is Race and Society Editor of the *New Statesman and New Society*

Richard Chirimuuta was born in Zimbabwe and is a freelance writer, specialising in African affairs. He is co-author of *Aids, Africa and Racism*

Jenny Hammond is Links Editor and Publications Worker for Third World First

Paul Martin is a Health Rights project worker, a member of the editorial group on *Health Matters* and Chair of Tower Hamlets Health Campaign

Dr Jihad Mashal is a Palestinian doctor in the Union of Palestinian Medical Relief Committees (UPMRC) in charge of one of its Health Centres in the Jordan valley

Lynda Medwell is treasurer of the Rongelap Resettlement Fund for the Nuclear-Free and Independent Pacific network

Dr Nerayo Tekle Michael is the coordinator of the Eritrean Public Health Programme

Frances O'Grady is a Health Rights project worker and is involved in research and campaigns around women's employment

Dr. Maire O'Shea, a psychiatrist with a psycho-social approach and a special interest in the mental health of ethnic minorities, has been involved for many years in therapeutic community work

Belinda Pratten is Chair of Health Rights, a member of the editorial group of *Health Matters*, a free-lance researcher on health issues and an ex-nurse

Luis Reveco is Administrator/Coodinator of Third World First

Wendy Savage is a Consultant in Obstetrics and Gynaecology at the London Hospital and author of *The Savage Enquiry: Who controls childbirth?*

INTRODUCTION

"Our hospitals belong to the people. They are a front of the revolution. Our hospitals are far more than centres dispensing medicine and cures. A hospital is a centre where our political line – that of serving the masses – is put into practice."

Samora Machel, Mozambique, 1971

Health is a political issue. In the West, however, we are encouraged to separate the *humanitarian* from the *political*. This distinction, itself ideological, obscures the politics behind health provision. Many people in the West take for granted a reasonable level of health and for them the World Health Organisation's (WHO) definition of health as '*complete physical, social and mental well-being*' is not so out of reach as it is for less fortunate sectors of our own society or for the oppressed majority in the Third World. For these people, the political struggle against multiple oppressions is the only way they can hope for a higher level of health for themselves and their children. Even in Britain it is increasingly difficult to ignore the 'health divide'. The long-term social and economic priorities which have led to this situation and the challenges to those priorities constitute the 'politics of health'.

Our own health system is mechanistic and curative. We tend to view the body as a machine, to think of health as the preserve of doctors and hospitals - a drugs and spare-parts service, and so define our own health needs in terms of ill-health. As a result, we also have a negative perception of health issues in the Third World. They are reduced by media stereotypes to the 'natural' disasters of famine-related deaths and epidemics, the 'natural' ill-health of extreme climates and exotic insects and bugs. But it is the *routine* experience of ill-health, as indicated by mortality and life expectancy rates, with its increased susceptibility to disease and premature death, which is the bottom line of underdevelopment, exploitation and the numerous oppressions of poverty. This is not natural. It is the result of long-term political and economic intervention.

In this, the West is implicated through the web of economic relationships by which the northern countries have become the beneficiaries of the wealth, raw materials and agricultural production of the Third World. More directly, the West subverts health through the irresponsible marketing policies of pharmaceutical companies, through nuclear technology and dumping, chemical pollution, export of inappropriate technologies and toxic substances.

Health issues cannot be considered separately from any of the issues of impoverishment caused by unequal power relations. For most of the world's people, the cause of poor health is poverty, the unequal distribution of land, knowledge and power. Half the world's people never see a trained health worker. One third are without clean water. A quarter of the world's children are malnourished. Yet the world spends $50 billion every three weeks on armaments. Recent studies in Britain have also drawn attention to the correlation between ill-health and inadequate housing, malnutrition, unemployment and poverty. Those most at risk from these problems are black people, Irish people and women. Wherever you look, the problem is not scarcity of resources, but their concentration in the hands of powerful groups. The solutions are political ones.

By helping people gain control over some aspect of their lives, community-based health programmes can be the catalyst for social change. In its fullest sense, primary health care is revolutionary. So it is not surprising that in most countries it has not been allowed to succeed. Governments have often reacted repressively, even brutally, against those promoting community health programmes. In Nicaragua under the dictator Somoza, in the Philippines under Marcos – as in Chile, Guatemala, Honduras and El Salvador today – a major attempt was made to suppress people- centred health schemes. Village health workers have become targets for attacks, torture and disappearances. In Nicaragua today, health posts and workers are a chief target of US-backed Contras. In Mozambique, health workers and posts are targets of the RENAMO terrorists sponsored by the South African government.

When the oppressed organise to liberate themselves from oppression, to claim a measure of self-determination over their own future – Cuba, Namibia, Nicaragua, Tigray, Eritrea are examples – then it is not surprising that community health is first on the agenda in the political process of equalising power and basic rights. In Britain too, both the NHS debate and examples like the Wendy Savage case have demonstrated the opposing priorities of high-tech curative care and a more participative, community-based approach. In Nicaragua and the Philippines, collective action promoted by community-based health programmes played a critical role in empowering people to overthrow dictators. In Eritrea and Tigray, the people's participation in programmes of health education, clinics, and preventive care has been an important element in peasant communities mobilising against the oppressive central government. Repressive regimes do have good reason to fear the empowering potential of community-directed health initiatives.

In the West, water and sanitation programmes did more to raise the general level of health than scientific discoveries or doctors, important though these may be. But now, in terms of our GNP and health expenditure, how well *are* we doing in Britain? If we want to find acceptable models for health priorities which involve the whole community, we can learn from certain Third World countries who, with relatively meagre resources, are implementing health programmes not as a privilege for some, but as a right for all. *Priorities* is another word for *politics*.

Jenny Hammond

WHO CARES FOR THE NHS?

A NUPE women's Day of Action against the proposed closure of the South London Hospital

The National Health Service is in crisis. HEALTH RIGHTS, working on a broad range of NHS and Public Health issues, argue that this crisis has been precipitated by a lack of resources and chronic underfunding, but behind it lie deeper and interrelated problems of organisation and structure. They call for more fundamental changes, in terms of democratisation and accountability and a shift of emphasis away from simply curing people when they are sick to making sure that they don't get sick in the first place.

BELINDA PRATTEN, PAUL MARTIN and FRANCES O'GRADY talk to Third World First.

3W1: *What do you think have been the achievements of the NHS?*

HR: The NHS has enabled a lot of people who wouldn't have had access to health care to get basic medical treatment. It has also redistributed wealth from the well and able-bodied to the sick and from the well-off to people who are worse off. Until recently, the NHS was a great success as a welfare state institution, but now it is facing a number of interrelated crises.

3W1: *How have these crises come about?*

HR: Their origins go back beyond Thatcher, to some extent, to the crisis in the welfare state in the mid 70s when cuts, moves towards increasing charges, and attacks on trade unions began. Since then, the ideology of the Thatcher government and cash limiting have intensified.
There are many subtle ways that the government is undermining the health service. The Tories' agenda is essentially the expansion of the private sector: increasing the amount of scope there is for making profit within the NHS for the private sector through privatisation. Things such as contracting out services increasingly erode public provision, for example wards are not as clean as they used to be. The development of internal markets within the NHS sets hospitals or areas against one another in terms of cost-cutting and the kind of service they are providing.

Over the last 10–15 years there has been a move towards more managerial control of the NHS and particularly so since the Griffiths report (1983) was introduced. There has always been a potential conflict between the needs of professionals, the needs of administrators and the needs of users and the users have always lost out on that. Local communities therefore have little or no say regarding the services they use. Decisions about what equipment to purchase and whether to develop more responsive services are taken by Health Service managers, representatives of the medical profession, and appointed Health Authority members.

Also the morale of staff has been deteriorating, not simply through cuts and low wages and through the threats of privatisation, but through the uncertainty and the lack of general commitment. There has been a spiral of demoralisation, and shortages of staff means that everyone is working at over-capacity. There is no way you can actually enjoy your work. It makes it very difficult.

3W1: *Will these trends affect some people more than others?*

HR: In the longer term if the economy continues to develop in the way that it is at the moment, then a two-tier health service will develop. This will obviously have dramatic impacts on the access of working class and black people to basic health care. Also, since the NHS is the largest employer in Europe, cuts in the NHS are going to have a bigger impact on unemployment among women, blacks and members of ethnic minorities. There is no doubt that as hospitals get rationalised into big central hospitals, working class areas in particular will be more affected because the bigger hospitals tend to be in middle class areas.

3W1: *You mentioned that the NHS was undemocratic. What did you mean by that?*

HR: The NHS was never conceived as something that would be in touch with ordinary people's lives. Its origins lie in the Poor Law institutions and voluntary hospitals which were in part paternalist institutions. The battle was basically lost when the NHS was set up. Because of the need to secure the settlement with the medical profession, the government chose to have it as something that was completely unelected.

But the NHS also has another part of its history located in people's struggles for a free, good, health care service, so there is always this conflict between the two and always a battle for supremacy between them.

3W1: *How does this affect women?*

HR: Women are the biggest workforce and the biggest users of health services. Yet very often the structure within the health service does not make it accessible to women. Women are defined as problematic in the first place. For example, child birth is defined as some kind of illness and something that needs to be controlled and managed by men rather than as something that is normal and can be controlled by women. We need to 'non-medicalise' womens' health.

It is again one of the contradictions of the NHS that in one sense it represents the success of people's struggle but in another it acts as a means of controlling, for example, women's fertility in terms of access to abortion and contraceptive facilities or in other cases, particularly in the case of black women, often forced control over fertility. Most

Gina Glover

Police lend their helmets in support of the nurses' protest at St. James Hospital, February 1988

women would like an NHS that really met our needs as we women define them and that
we had real control over.

3W1: *What are your views on the use of high technology in medicine?*

HR: The golden rule when considering this technology is whether it has been evaluated
and is safe. By these criteria, many drug therapies and new high-tech medical facilities
and surgical techniques would be very questionable. We would like to see the fostering
of more appropriate health technologies, not necessarily in a low-tech sense but simply
trying to assess new technology in a much more general way, not on a cost benefit
analysis. A lot of technology is inappropriate and has taken control away from users, for
example women during childbirth.

It is also worth pointing out that there is a conflict between the profit motive and
people's needs and that is why so many inappropriate technologies are developed. In a
world where people had control over the health care system the design and production of
technologies and drugs would be very different.

3W1: *Is racism a factor within the NHS do you think?*

HR: It operates in two ways. Black people are both workers and users. They are in the
worst paid jobs and they receive the worst care – often a care that isn't responsive to
their needs.

There are many examples of racism in the health service, whether it is to do with the
sterilisation of black women or genetic screening or mental health provision. One
important issue at the moment is the campaigns run in Hackney against black people
being asked to show their passports before they are given access to health. Black people
are treated as if they are not citizens. There are also the wider issues of tackling the real
causes of ill-health, the poverty that black people suffer disproportionately, and the

racism in the health service both in terms of provision and employment.

One concern about employment is the historical recruitment of black women into the SEN (State Enrolled Nurse) as opposed to SRN (State Registered Nurse) scheme, which is for white women. It is just crude racial segregation. There is great concern that changes in the nursing structure will reproduce this segregation and again black women will carry out the generalised caring duties and white women will be bought off with 'being allowed' to take on more medicalised skills.

The NHS is in many ways institutionally racist from top to bottom both in its employment and in its other practices. An equal opportunities approach to promotion or training or facilities provided would be a start. But only a wider awareness of racism, the adoption of an anti-racist strategy and the self-organisation of black groups will bring real progress.

3W1: *What are your main priorities for change in the NHS?*

HR: We would like to see the NHS improved on the basis of promoting equality, particularly for groups who at the moment don't have adequate health services or adequate access to health services. It would be based within a 'rights' framework, both individual rights and collective rights to health care. Obviously more resources should be given to health care. Britain doesn't spend that much, relatively speaking, on health care services. We would want to see a shift of emphasis away from simply curing people when they are sick to making sure that they don't get sick in the first place.

In some senses it is a political question as well, of giving people the opportunity to have more influence over how health services are developed in this country, both for the workers who provide the service and for the people who use those services. It is about shifting the balance and changing the whole way health is conceptualised from a medical to a more non-medical model and also increasing participation in the health service.

I think we are seeing the emergence of a new approach to health which places it in a broad social and economic perspective. It has been crystallised, if you like, in the WHO's Health For All programmes and in its health promotion work. Essentially it links health and well-being to poverty, to employment, to housing and to all the daily things that touch our lives. I think that is an exciting movement. It stresses community participation, community development and non-medical models of health. So, it is actually providing quite a challenge and a positive vision of the way forward.

One of the most obvious things we must guard against is the Edwina Curry version of health which is to 'victim blame' and to individualise the causes of ill-health and present only individual solutions. We want to ensure the real causes of ill-health are very firmly located in economic and social causes: poverty, unemployment, bad housing, racism, sexism and the environment. Governments must not be allowed to get off the hook.

3W1: *What are the prospects for change?*

HR: Because of the health service crisis there has been a lot of spontaneous grassroots activity around the cuts. Since the late 70s there has been a growth in the community health movement. This has been influenced by feminism and radicalised. It is now posing quite strong challenges on a local level to how services are delivered and the types of relationships that are encouraged and fostered by those services. It covers anything from women's health groups, mental health groups, carers, self-health groups around certain illnesses. It is very diverse and spontaneous.

In the early 80s it was the community groups, particularly women's groups, who were actually saying that they didn't simply want *more* health services, and began qualifying the *types* of services that they wanted. That has been a very strong critical influence from a radical perspective on the NHS.

Interestingly, the trend since the early 70s has been for greater organisation of workers within the health service. The health service workers' dispute this year showed quite a change in the type of action that had been envisaged. It was much more grassroots and more spontaneous and, in that sense, exciting. A lot of workers who might not have been expected to come out and defend the NHS came out because it wasn't simply about pay and conditions. It was about the broader issues. The action showed a sort of radicalism and a militancy not seen before, certainly among nurses.

One of the interesting features of industrial struggle over the last few years is the development of a relationship between workers' struggles and the community and I think there is obviously a lot of potential there. The creation of the dialogue between the users of the service and the workers in that service ought to be dynamite really! Some of the action has been successful - the government has been made to back off in many ways. That is quite incredible, that what is seen as a very weak and disorganised, predominantly female workforce should actually succeed in ways that other sectors haven't. That is exciting.

What would be good over the years to come is to see the strengthening between the community and health service workers, so that when the workers do come out on strike in the health service they don't lose the support of the users of the service. That is one of the most important issues in terms of industrial strategies for the Health Service. In that sense the recent disputes showed the strength of feeling among health workers and non-health workers for the defence of the NHS and that is very encouraging since there is always going to be that block of support which is going to be a major problem for the government in the future.

A study comparing the health of people in Divis flats with the new housing estate of Twinbrook found that residents reported:

Health Problem	Divis	Twinbrook
Longstanding illness or disability	33% adults	16% adults
Longstanding illness or infirmity	21% children	7% children
Health not good (self reporting)	29% men	6.5% men
Health not good (self reporting)	38% women	1% women

Source: *Housing and Health in West Belfast* **Blackman, Evason et al University of Ulster for Divis Joint Development Committee**

Chris Taylor / 3W1

RACISM AND THE MENTAL HEALTH OF BLACK PEOPLE IN BRITAIN

Why are black people in Britain so proportionately over-represented in mental institutions? Why are they five times more likely to receive custodial treatment? YASMIN ALIBHAI challenges the racism inherent in the treatment black people receive in our society and in our mental institutions.

13

The mad look in Nusrat Begum's eyes gets more and more evident each year. She spends most days ripping up the carpets and floorboards in her flat and chopping up furniture, even the precious kitchen cabinets she saved up for a year to buy.

Forty years old, she came here as a young widow from Pakistan with her two children, one of whom is mentally retarded and violent. She

**The logo of NAFSIYAT
('body, mind and spirit')
the Inter-Cultural Therapy Centre**

lives with her father. He is senile and registers nothing of the world, pushing trollies around the streets. There is hardly any money in the house. Nusrat has attacked the neighbours and hammered holes in their walls. She has been sectioned twice, and is frequently to be seen being hauled away in police vans, screaming sometimes, laughing sometimes, like in a Ken Russell

film. Her doctor knows nothing about her home life and the fact that she cracked up soon after her mother, who was her prime support, died. The consultant psychiatrist at one of the country's largest mental hospitals has little time for Nusrat because she *"speaks no English* [which in fact she does] *and obviously has cultural problems adjusting to life here"*. He gives her plenty of tablets, which she never takes. No community psychiatric nurse has ever visited her.

What is happening to Nusrat is happening to thousands of black and Asian people in Britain and the statistics speak for themselves. When compared to white people, they are proportionately over-represented in mental institutions, are five times more likely to receive custodial treatment (often enforced), twice as likely to have their first diagnoses changed, see junior staff, and receive physical treatment instead of therapy. It is not surprising, therefore, that so many people see the mental health services as another arm of the racist criminal justice system - where section 136 of the Mental Health Act is used as a social control mechanism to incarcerate young black men in particular. After all, the prisons are full. A recent MIND report confirms this view: *"Possible racism inherent in the police and psychiatric profession could be a factor in these disturbing statistics"*.

The statistics are also disturbing indicators of how society uses and abuses mental illness against those people it considers 'aliens', 'outsiders' or threateningly 'abnormal'. When the society is as vociferously racist – and increasingly so – as Britain is, the implications for mentally ill black people are obvious. Psychiatry has a specific role in creating concepts of conformity and assimilation. And then there is always the uneasy line between dissent and illness. In most cases this is not overtly planned. The point is that subconsciously, to white practitioners and the white state, a black person who is mad, is by definition, *madder* and potentially more violent. This is true of offenders too. The entire criminal justice system perceives black offenders as intrinsically more dangerous than white criminals. As one young Rastafarian woman who was depressed and institutionalised as schizophrenic said, *"They look frightened when they see you – even though they have power, and they treated me as if I was a killer or something – you know, not looking into my eyes at all".*

And where do these perceptions come into the national consciousness from? History has prepared the white natives of this country well for these attitudes. One of the many justifications used for the appalling institutions of slavery and colonialism was that black people were less than human, adolescents in arrested states of development, childlike, credulous, over-physical, beastly, mad even. Jung and Freud in their writings showed the same attitudes, exposing the way the entire discipline of psychotherapy is corrupted by these irrational beliefs. Jung, for example wrote, *"Living with the barbaric races exerts a suggestive influence on the laboriously tamed instincts of the white race and tends to pull it down".* Whether expressed in the daily papers or implied in the kind of 'help' black people are given in the health service when they are mentally and emotionally distressed, these attitudes and perceptions continue to underscore what is said and done.

The central issue is one of power. Mental health professionals are dealing with the most powerless people in the community. They hold the ultimate weapon, the power to lock someone up under the Mental Health Act. In individual interactions, the relationship between the patient and the practitioner can be intolerably uneven. Add to this the processes of race and class prejudice and the situation can and often does completely victimise the black patient. This issue of power is seldom addressed within the area of mental health. Instead compensatory measures are taken when dealing with disadvantaged groups, or their 'culture' is pathologised. For example, there is a group of white practitioners in Bradford who talk about their "poor Asians", lost through dislocation and migration.

Age-specific rates of admissions with a diagnosis of schizophrenia or paranoia in England per 100,000 population in 1981

Age Group	Admissions			
	First		All	
	England	Caribbean	England	Caribbean
A. MALES				
16 - 24	17	82	64	386
25 - 34	17	95	137	617
35 - 44	13	17	113	266
45 - 65	8	22	69	112
66+	7	—	25	55
B. FEMALES				
16 - 24	8	19	37	153
25 - 34	11	43	81	259
35 - 44	10	35	96	271
45 - 65	15	39	125	234
66+	12	30	44	64

Source: Cochrane and Singh Bal, *Mental hospital rates of immigrants to England: a comparison of 1971 and 1981*

"I have always believed that there is a very unequal power relationship between a health giver and receiver. The structures of the profession are all based on that particular power relationship. In mental health, that power assumes frightening proportions because you can lock people up at the stroke of a pen."

Jafar Kareem *New Society 6/5/88*

They do not explore why it is that the group that is increasingly being decanted into mental institutions consists of young black Britons born here. This group, who don't have the core that their parents brought with them when they migrated, have been exposed to this racist soci-

15

ety from the time they were born and it has destroyed them.

The other question which is still being neglected in the field of mental health treatment is the role of the 'curer'. Do they teach black people to manage their pain of living in a racist society, and keep the status quo, or do they encourage them to feel empowered, so that they can challenge the structures which have dehumanised them? This brings in the red rag of *politicisation* of a profession that has traditionally not even slightly swayed while sitting on the non-committed fence it has always sat on. But, in order to understand and be understood in the black psyche, there needs to be an acknowledgement of those external realities, and a body of theory which can be used in analysis and which moves beyond the domestic reasons for damage to a person into the area of racism as a causative factor in mental illness, both for blacks and whites.

In practical terms this means looking at the transference mechanisms that could take place, say, when a white therapist or psychiatrist is dealing with a black patient and vice versa. How do both deal with the heat of confronting racism – and use that as a therapeutic tool? Other factors also matter. To what extent is it relevant to talk about nuclear families, when there are so many examples of different notions of child rearing, multiple parenting and selfhood? Blood is not always thicker than water – in many situations, relationships are much thicker than blood.

And it is all these issues – so important in an increasingly international world – that organisations like Nafsiyat, an inter-racial therapy group in London, and the Transcultural Therapy Group, are trying to tackle. They are fighting all the complacency and assumptions they have found to operate in the field. They are forcing outside issues like racism into the consultancy room, acknowledged not only as the product of insane fevered imaginations, but as an actuality which at least in part has caused the mental illness, and most certainly influenced the treatment that is available to black people. They see the savagery of colonialism continuing and destroying not only the material well-being of subject people, but destroying the very kernel of their existence and identity. Jafar Kareem, director of Nafsiyat, believes that it is impossible to practice psychotherapy without a philosophy of equality underpinning it, and that talking about

> *"Let's be very clear. It is not because there are more mad people among the ethnic minorities, or that because there are ethnic minorities there is a problem. Just the reverse. We are looking at a section of the community who are not getting a fair deal."*
>
> **Jafar Kareem. New Society 6/5/88**

inter-cultural therapy without talking about racism is equally impossible. Most white practitioners freeze at the very word racism. Why? Nafsiyat is involved in examining these issues and many others, like the status problem, when black therapists are rejected by white and black patients as representing an inferior service, and why certain manifestations of behaviour are considered with more disapprobation than others?

In other radical organisations, like the White City Project, workers are examining the role of mental health organisations in a hardening capitalist society, and looking clearly at the issue of race and class as compound oppressions that produce the worst injustices. The effect of oppression and disadvantage which leads to poor housing and unemployment can no longer be excluded from the tranquillity of the consulting rooms of mental health practitioners. The world is too tumultuous, internally and externally, for black people, for this luxurious blindness to continue.

Nusrat Begum's life, as it burns itself out through her red eyes, should be a reminder that the way she is being treated is simply unacceptable in a society that still pretends to be the most civilised nation in the world.

COLONIAL LEGACIES: The mental health of the Irish in Britain

Colonialism, economic exploitation and the racist attitudes to justify them go hand in hand. MAIRE O'SHEA argues that it is impossible to separate the stress which has given rise to mental illness among Irish people in Britain from issues of Irish colonial experience at the hands of the British.

Joanne O'Brien / Format

Overcrowding and the stress of city life contribute to the pressures on new arrivals

Research carried out in the late 70s by Raymond Cochrane, Professor of Psychology at Birmingham University, and recently brought up to date, has shown that the Irish in Britain have the highest rate of admission to mental hospitals of all ethnic minority groups and two-and-a-half times the British rate. High suicide rates have provided additional evidence of unacceptable levels of distress.

The lack of response of academics and of the Transcultural Psychiatry Society to the issue of the mental health of the Irish, the largest ethnic minority in Britain, has been disappointing. Only Cochrane has included the Irish in a survey of the incidents of mental hospital admissions among ethnic minority groups in Britain. His 1971 figures (Cochrane 1977) are about to be published again in a comparative study with 1981 figures.

He found (see Table) that in 1971 those born in the six occupied counties had the highest rate at 1,242. Those born in the Republic of Ireland came next at 1,110. He was surprised that the Irish, whom he saw as having fewer "transitions" to make on arrival in Britain, were more vulnerable than the Asians who have many transitions to make. To explain the high Irish admission rate he postulated several options: a greater propensity for hospitalisation as a response to mental illness; an inherent vulnerability to mental illness in the Irish culture and the destruction of Irish society and personality by colonialism. The genetic factor he dismissed for lack of evidence. He viewed Irish emigration as a dual phenomenon with the high rate of mental illness accounted for by a significant minority on the margins of the community who have emigrated to escape personal problems centering around alcohol, but in fact bring the problems with them.

17

In 1981, although figures for Irish admissions had decreased, they were still higher than other groups and those for the Irish Republic had overtaken Northern Ireland. High rates among the Irish are accounted for by high rates of alcoholism and schizophrenia, although the rate of schizophrenia admissions is higher among Afro-Caribbeans.

The findings of his subsequent community survey conflict with the results of a community survey carried out by Anthony Clare (unpublished thesis) who found excessively high rates of depression and anxiety, but not of schizophrenia. Cochrane's view of the majority of the Irish

"You always told jokes about the Englishman, the Scotsman and the Irishman, didn't you ? It's not about the Englishman, the Irishman and the Scotsman any more, it's just the Irishman, isn't it? I think they are pretty cruel today. I think the problems in Northern Ireland have changed the whole situation. When a bombing or anything like that happens I say, 'Thank God for supermarkets', because you don't have to speak, you don't have to ask for a loaf of bread. I do feel intimidated. I wouldn't want to get into a difficult situation, because I wouldn't know how I'd react. When I buy *The Irish Post* I fold it over when I am in the shop - and I like to buy it in an Indian shop. I notice myself doing those things, very much so.
The English don't try to understand Irish people. But then they've learnt nothing. They don't realise that they have lived in so many countries and they have only tried to wipe out the ways of the people there, and stamp their way on the country. They are a very lonely people among themselves, they have no culture."

Nancy Lyons in *Across the Water: Irish Women's Lives in Britain*, by Mary Lennon, Marie McAdam, and Joanne O'Brien. Virago 1988

community, as successful and well-integrated into the host society, also conflicts with the figures relating to two London boroughs, which show that the Irish have the highest rate of unemployment, low wages, homelessness and substandard accommodation. Nationwide the Irish have the lowest rate of home ownership.

Cochrane's interpretation of these figures has been disputed. They show that the Irish community are more likely to be diagnosed as suffering from schizophrenia and alcohol-related psychosis. Other writers have argued that this has less to do with an Irish propensity towards mental illness than with inadequate understanding of emigration by the host society, compounded by dubious referral and diagnostic practices. He omits from consideration important factors: the inclusion of racism in the policies of admitting agencies; and the disinclination of the client to seek help at an early stage due to distrust of alien professionals. The latter could well also have played a part in the denial of psychological distress by the Irish interviewed in the community survey.

What can be done?

In 1985 a group of Irish professionals concerned about the lack of sensitivity in the statutory services to these findings, organised a public meeting in Brent. The Brent Irish Mental Health Group was set up to highlight the special problems faced by Irish People. A report on the mental health of the Irish in the area found that the most vulnerable groups were single men and married women. Unemployment, high rates of homelessness and poor housing conditions, low pay and poor working conditions, cultural problems and racism were all contributory factors. The Group has since published a booklet containing interviews with Irish users of the psychiatric services which has a complete bibliography of the very limited research available. One local Social Services office has begun to monitor their Irish clientele.

In January 1987, the Irish in Britain Representation Group (IBRG) in Camden organised a national conference to explore, with members of the Irish community, the reasons for the appall-

Age standardised rates for all admissions for all diagnoses by country of birth, in England and Wales (1971) and England (1981), per 100,000 population

Country of Birth	Rates per 100,000 population					
	1971			1981		
	M	F	All	M	F	All
England	434	551	494	418	583	504
Scotland	712	679	695	740	847	797
N.Ireland	1391	1102	1242	793	880	838
Irish Republic	1065	1153	1110	1054	1102	1080
Caribbean	449	621	539	565	532	548
India	368	436	403	317	326	321
Pakistan	294	374	336	259	233	245
Germany	356	513	439	280	470	379
Italy	272	400	340	293	421	360
USA	359	576	473	314	251	281

Source: Cochrane and Singh Bal, *Mental hospital rates of immigrants to England: a comparison of 1971 and 1981*

ingly high rate of mental hospital admissions, to draw the attention of the statutory services to the special problems of the Irish and to attract funding for pilot projects. This successful conference attracted over 200 mainly Irish people with a preponderance of psychiatric professionals and consumers. The decision was taken to set up a forum on the mental health of the Irish, at first meeting in London but later in other centres.

This forum now meets monthly. It has analysed the political and cultural dimensions of Irish emotional distress and aims to provide space for Irish people to explore their own feelings about being Irish in Britain. It is working for an input into the statutory psychiatric services and into professional training programmes. It is seeking funding for a "drop-in" centre with facilities for counselling and group work and aims to have a research, as well as a therapeutic, function.

Hospital admission rates confirm that there are also high levels of distress in both Northern Ireland and in the Republic. In my view, the psychological problems of the Irish in Ireland and of Irish emigrants to Britain have to be considered in the context of 800 years of colonial experi-

ence. There have been two episodes of genocide: the first by massacre under Cromwell, followed by mass deportations to Barbados and the driving of the remaining dispossessed into the mountainous areas of the western seaboard; the second through famine in the 1840s deliberately engineered by the imperial power forcing the export of corn when the potatoes had been destroyed by blight. Under the 18th century penal laws, it was a criminal offence for Catholics to own property. They were barred from professions and the colonial parliament; they had no vote; the only education was in illegal "hedge" schools. The foundations of the power of the Catholic church in Ireland were laid when Catholic priests were sheltered from persecution by the people who in turn were comforted by promises of happiness in the hereafter. The Irish colonial experience differs from that of the people of the Indian subcontinent, for example, in that the fabric of Indian society was left intact and the native rulers used to underpin the imperial power, while the entire fabric of Irish society was destroyed and the rebellious educated elite killed or driven out, leaving the priests to take their places.

Racist attitudes have been inculcated from the earliest periods of British intervention in Ireland. The works of Geraldus Cambrensis, a 14th century clerical scholar, contained the first recorded propagation of racist stereotypes to justify colonisation, after the Pope himself had given his blessing to the Norman Conquest of Ireland in a special Bull. He depicts the Irish as having the facial features of monkeys, coarse hair, bandy legs and pot bellies due to idleness and overindulgence, as being wild, uncouth and given to savage fighting. This stereotype has persisted to the present day.

The racism of the whole colonial experience was internalised over generations and carried to Britain by the emigrants. In addition to the trauma of emigration per se, they were then faced with the pressures of being Irish and living in the territory of colonial power still occupying part of their country and for the past 19 years waging a colonial war against their people in the six occupied counties.

Those who came to Britain in the mass migration of the 40s and 50s, recruited as cheap labour in a time of labour shortage, had been disillusioned by the failure of native governments since 1922 to provide a decent living for them in their own country. The immigrants felt rejected

---

The colonial background
Health Statistics for the North of Ireland

"The level of new out-patients seen in hospitals here for mental handicap and mental illness in 1982 was 51% and 16% higher than in England."
Developing Hospital Services E.H.S.S.B.1984

"An average of almost twice as many work days are lost through illness here compared with England."
Minister of Health and Social Services (N.L.) 1-6-86

---

and at the same time guilty about leaving. No longer seeing uniformed British forces on the streets of the 26 counties, many could not blame British imperialism for their survival in the neo-colonial subsistence economy. Those who came from the occupied six counties to escape from discrimination and repression felt abandoned by the 26 county Irish state. In Britain they were mainly confined to work too badly paid or too heavy for the British.

The current wave of emigration has brought a different type of Irish immigrant to Britain. These are in the main the young people under 25 from the towns who grew up in the brief period of economic expansion and improved public services, with second level education and high expectations. Some are unmarried mothers or

battered wives who have suffered in Ireland from inadequate protection from violent husbands. They are converging on London where low-level jobs are available, but most are reduced to living in squats or sleeping rough.

They were faced with anti-Irish racism which escalated in the early 70s when Britain had begun to wage war against the nationalist people of the six counties. Anti-Irish jokes reappeared. After the Birmingham bombings the Irish were attacked by mobs and burnt out of their houses. Irish political meetings were attacked by the NF. The Prevention of Terrorism Act silenced protest against British atrocities in Ireland, criminalised the entire Irish community, excluded them from political activities and instilled fear of any assertion of Irishness. It has led to family breakdown due to suspicion and scapegoating. Victims have suffered psychological damage, from chronic anxiety and depression to paranoid psychosis. The Irish have been faced with the spectacle of increasing collaboration with British imperial forces by their 'sovereign' government, culminating in the present time in the extradition of Irish republicans to a British judicial system from which Irish people can expect no justice.

Perfumes, cosméticos e medicamentos em sua porta.

WARNING:
PHARMABUSINESS CAN SERIOUSLY DAMAGE YOUR HEALTH

Third World First is joining efforts with other organisations to campaign for more responsible research, production and marketing of drugs in poor countries and at home. LUIS REVECO and CHRIS TAYLOR argue that the pressure of the present debt crises on health and education budgets makes the adoption of a rational use of an essential drugs policy more urgent than ever in all poor countries.

In 1977 the World Health Organisation compiled the List of Essential Drugs (LED) containing only 220 drugs which together were sufficient to treat all diseases. WHO defined four characteristics for a drug to be 'essential':

- they should meet real medical needs
- they should have significant therapeutic value
- they should be acceptably safe
- they should offer satisfactory value for money

Since the first publication of LED, the pharma-industry has maintained consistent opposition to the whole concept. In 1978, the International Federation of Pharmaceutical Manufacturers Associations (IFPMA), which represents virtually all of the world's major pharmaceutical companies, was less than enthusiastic about the essential drug list and called the medical and economic arguments for such a list *"fallacious"* and said that adopting it *"could result in suboptimal medical care and might reduce health standards"*. In 1984, the Association of British Pharmaceutical Industries (ABPI) launched a major campaign to oppose the introduction of a limited list of drugs for the NHS. The industry took full-page advertisements in leading newspapers, campaigned vigorously within the health professions, claimed the measures would take away doctors' freedom to prescribe, and would ultimately lead to the destruction of the pharmaceutical industry. Throughout 1986 and 1987, pharmaceutical associations in Nigeria, India, Philippines, Bolivia, Argentina, Italy and Netherlands have all protested strongly against attempts to introduce a LED.

The List of Essential Drugs has, however, stood the test of time. More than 80 countries in the Third World have adopted the LED to their requirements. In 1982, the Bangladeshi government removed unnecessary drugs from the market and devised its own list of 150 essential drugs plus 76 products for specialist use. Eritrea and Nicaragua, among other countries, have followed the same example and now produce a large proportion of their own essential drugs.

Despite vehement opposition from pharmabusiness, health professionals and even some Western governments, the rational policy of having a LED has slowly won support. Its advantages are clear. Many poor countries have been spending 20–30% of their meagre national health budgets on drug imports, and still the larger proportion of the population cannot get the most needed drugs. A rational List of Essential Drugs can go a long way to remedying this situation.

Meanwhile, the pharmaceutical industry continues to defend its massive profits accumulation by opposing the introduction of Essential Drugs Lists. WHO estimates that some $500

For the price of this tonic, an Indian family could have bought all the nutritious food shown here.

million have been invested to support national drug programmes to overcome essential drug shortages. However, this is only about 5% of the amount being spent by the pharmaceutical industry to promote new drugs.

The Therapeutic Jungle

Health workers and consumers are faced with a confusing therapeutic jungle, an overwhelming number of unnecessary, unhelpful and sometimes unavailable drugs. This jungle is fertilised by ignorance, much of which is provided by the pharmaceutical industry in order to ensure profits continue to increase.

The pharmaceutical industry is flooding the world with drugs which are useless or which do not address the specific health needs of the country concerned. A US AID study in 1981 concluded that as many as 70% of the drugs on the world market are inessential and/or undesirable products. A UN study in 1984 found that in Mexico, Kenya and Malaysia, the drugs marketed by foreign transnational pharmaceutical companies *did not correspond to the major health requirements and priorities of each country*. In all three countries, the best selling products were vitamins and tonics, despite the different disease patterns in each country.

It is a pattern repeated over and over again throughout the world. Nearly 18% of all drug imports in North Yemen in 1980 were for vitamins and tonics, compared to only 1% for drugs to treat the country's three most widespread diseases. In Sri Lanka in 1977, aspirins, vitamins and tonics accounted for over 50% of pharmaceutical production. In Nepal, in 1980, more than 30% of the drugs on the market were tonics. The effects of this upon public health are clear. As a Filipino health worker put it: "We continue to see Rural Health Units stocked with useless drugs, while deficient when it comes to much-needed life-saving drugs such as antibiotics."

This policy by pharmabusiness of dumping useless drugs, can also be a significant drain upon a nation's scarce economic resources. The Bangladesh government found that one third of the money spent on drugs during 1981 was for unnecessary and useless medicines, such as tonics, vitamin mixtures, cough elixirs, and hundreds of similar compounds. Over 70% of the Bangladesh drugs market was controlled by multinational firms, so money was being drained from the country to pay for useless drugs.

A major problem is often the shortage of the most essential drugs. A study in Kinshasa, the capital of Zaire, in 1982, showed that multinational drug companies have a great impact on the quality of treatment offered by neighbourhood health clinics and pharmacies. These routinely lacked essential drugs while they stocked hazardous and expensive drugs. Before the Essential Drugs Programme began in Kenya, it was estimated in 1985 that up to 25% of rural health centres were closed at any one time due to drug shortages.

Study after study shows the inappropriateness of 'poly-pharmacy' treatment of much drug prescribing and the over-medication which results. The main cause of poor prescribing practice is the dependence of health workers on the pharmaceutical industry for information about drugs.

Depo-Provera

But dumping does not just involve useless or inappropriate drugs. It can also include dangerous ones as the case of Depo-Provera shows. Depo-Provera (or DP) is an injectable contraceptive which was developed in the mid-60s by the US drug company, Upjohn. After investigation by the US Food and Drug Administration, it was found that DP was linked with a wide range of side effects ranging from nausea, depression and loss of periods to heavy bleeding and possibly cancer of the breast, cervix and the uterus wall. Eventually the use of DP was banned in the USA.

Upjohn compensated by marketing DP elsewhere. On their own admission, Upjohn spent over $4.2m during the 70s as bribes for government and hospital employees *"for the purpose of*

Advertising in the Third World puts enormous pressure on the poor to spend precious income on ineffective or dangerous drugs.

obtaining sales". DP was portrayed as a quick and easy form of contraception since it requires a single 150mg injection every 3 months. As a result it was seen as positive by some women users. Hari John, a woman doctor from India, explains:

"Most forms of contraception are very difficult to hide, and DP is the only one their husbands won't know about. Using DP is the only way these women can have control over any aspect of their lives".

By 1978 it was estimated that between three and five million women worldwide were using DP. Many were not told of the possible effects upon their health. Some were not even told they were being given the drug. In fact there is evidence to suggest that women in the Third World together with black, working-class and mentally-ill women in Britain were used to test the drug. An Upjohn official is quoted as saying that

the issue of DP's side-effects *"can only be resolved by exposing humans"* to it.

But DP is not an isolated case. As Josie Ziani, a Malaysian activist has pointed out: *"Untested and dangerous contraceptives are dumped on a massive scale on women in many Third World countries, disabling millions"*.

This merely demonstrates the racist and sexist double standards used by pharmabusiness to test and sell drugs in the Third World which are defined as unsafe in the West. And all in the pursuit of fast profits

Drugging the 'Third World'

The basic philosophy behind pharmabusiness has been to sell what it can, where it can, for the highest price it can get. Increasingly, drug companies are targeting poor countries where legislation governing drug safety is often less stringent than in the West.

During 1985, the ten most profitable pharmaceutical transnationals recorded profit margins on drugs sales ranging from 27% to 43%. In contrast, in the UK, the ten most profitable automotive concerns recorded profit margins ranging from 2% to 10%; the ten most profitable building and construction enterprises, 3% to 8%; the ten most profitable brewers and distilleries, 8% to 15%; and the ten most profitable electronic firms, 4% to 22%.

These massive profits are gained by a global pattern of aggressive marketing, racist testing and dumping of unsafe drugs, extortionate overpricing and notorious dirty-dealings. According to the UN Centre on Transnational Corporations, by the year 2000, sales in Africa, Asia and Latin America will increase to some 48% of the world total, while sales in Europe and North America are predicted to decline to only some 39% of the world market. Subsidiaries of multinational pharmaceutical companies control a major share of the market in most developing countries. In India, Glaxo established a subsidiary in 1914 with a capital of 150,000 rupees. By 1971, it was worth Rs.72 million, of which Rs.54 million was owned by foreign shareholders. In one single year, the Indian subsidiary sent Rs.3.2 million in payments to the parent company in England. In other words, both the Indian workforce and consumers are providing a substantial income for the UK multinational and its shareholders.

No Money – No Drugs

A study in 1980 of the market in South-East Asia found final retail prices of drugs marked up by as much as 300% on the import cost. In Bangladesh, during 1981, UK manufacturers were charging five times the market price for raw materials to their subsidiaries on specific drugs. In Argentina, over-pricing by transnational subsidiaries was found to range from 143% to 3,700%, while in Colombia, in 1970, the degree of overpricing ranged from 350% to 6,500% of the international market prices. As many drugs

are significantly over-priced, it is the poor who suffer most.

For ten years now, pharmabusiness has paid lip-service to the essential drugs concept while in practice it has consistently sought to undermine the application of that concept.

Drug safety and prices will continue to be a major issue, as governments and the public try to get the best possible value for their scarce health budgets. Better training and better information about drugs and their proper roles in health care will be the topic of continuing debate. Improvements in the distribution of drugs, specially in the rural areas of poor countries, will be an ongoing concern. But the central issue will revolve around the problem of which drugs and how many. The question of limiting the number of drugs on the market and better focusing of research towards real innovation is a debate that must be resolved, if a healthy pharmaceutical industry is to be achieved.

There is no single answer to the complex question of the 'pharmaceutical jungle'. Simple steps are being, and have been, taken in many countries to improve the rational use of essential drugs. More and more people are demanding both better health and the rational use of drugs. The past ten years have seen the beginning of positive changes. Dr Halfdan Mahler, Director General of WHO, states:

"Thirty years ago modern health technology had just awakened and was full of promise. Since then, its expansion has surpassed all dreams, only to become a nightmare. For it has become over-sophisticated and over-costly. It is dictating our health policies unwisely; and what is useful is being applied to too few. Based on these technologies, a huge medical industry has grown up with powerful vested interests of its own. Like the sorceror's apprentice, we have lost control - social control – over health technology. The slave of our imagination has become the master of our creativity. We must now learn to control it again and use it wisely, in the struggle for health freedom. This struggle is important for all countries; for developing countries it is crucial."

AIDS, SEXUAL POLITICS AND SECTION 28

MAUREEN OLIVER of the Organisation for Lesbian and Gay Action (OLGA) comments on the dangerous hypocrisies and threats to everybody's health inherent in the infamous section 28 of the recently enacted Local Government Bill.

It is clear from the wording of Section 28 that part of the background to this discriminatory piece of legislation is the AIDS crisis, an unpleasant feature of which has been the reaction of some of our press and media who delight in the worst kind of sensational journalism. They have mounted what can only be described as a virulent and savage anti-Gay attack as a response to the growing alarm in the country. As a result, Lesbians and Gays have been targeted for abuse and hostility.

That Lesbians are among the lowest risk group for AIDS/HIV infection has been ignored, while information about possible risks for the heterosexual community has been obscured. This atmosphere provided the ground for the seeds of prejudice and ignorance that made Section 28 possible.

The Conservative government's campaign has sought to erect a fantasy family, consisting of a white middle class man and woman and two neat,clean, tidy, orderly children, that requires protection against the supposed onslaught of 'seditious' homosexual material 'promoted' in schools by certain Labour-controlled councils. This image hardly reflects the lives of ordinary people in this country today. All that the 'positive images' campaign in one or two boroughs sought to achieve was increased tolerance of an oppressed minority that has no effective protection in law in this country and has suffered press scapegoating.

This is all the more cynical when the government is seen to be discriminating quite openly against families in its introduction of such measures as the Poll Tax – which threatens to cause parents to evict children to avoid harsh taxation – and its continued policy of unemployment that drives family wage-earners in the North to leave home to find work.

The recent Immigration Act is tearing apart Black and ethnic minority families by repatriating their members, some of whom have been resident in this country for as long as 25 years. Destruction of the NHS contributes further to the suffering of families, and the new Social Security Act and the Housing legislation bring further misery and deprivation to those who do not conform to their wealthy middle class stereotype.

More sinisterly the attempt by the government to reinforce the myth that it is Lesbians and Gay men who abuse children, totally ignores the recent findings about child sex abuse. In fact, according to the recent NSPCC report, 97% of all child sex abuse is perpetrated by heterosexual men upon girls.

The threat to our families is further compounded by the fact that the excellent work done by groups such as the Terence Higgins Trust on the dissemination of vital AIDS information is being hampered by the subtle effects of Section 28. Asked whether their work had been affected, Simon Pollard of that organisation said many local authorities, fearing prosecution, had expressed reluctance to use the group's material. By restricting the necessary education of our young people concerning safer sex, the government is placing in danger the future of all children in this country.

A recent Sunday Telegraph attack on the work of the Terence Higgins Trust, entitled 'Is there a homosexual plot?', claimed that, by emphasising that AIDS is also a problem for heterosexuals, the group was merely trying to offload responsibility from the Lesbian and Gay community. Such misinformation is obviously highly dangerous given the clear evidence that AIDS is spreading among heterosexuals and that the incidence among both heterosexuals and homosexuals is randomly distributed and differs from area to area.

The Terence Higgins Trust's work and that of other AIDS charities should not be undervalued. It is vital that such groups continue unhindered by the worst excesses of this government's attack on the Lesbian and Gay community. We at OLGA will continue to fight section 28 as long as it takes. We stress that Lesbian and Gay Rights are Human Rights.

AIDS, IMPERIALISM AND RACISM

RICHARD CHIRIMUUTA, co-author of *Aids, Africa and Racism*, discusses the hysterical and sensationalised reaction in Western Europe and the US to the AIDS pandemic which reveals a deep racism that threatens efforts to understand and control the disease.

Jean Fraser

Manchester, 20 February 1988. Protests against clause 28 generated huge public support

Since the days of slavery black people have been stereotyped as dirty, disease ridden and sexually promiscuous, and it came as no surprise that the Acquired Immune Deficiency syndrome, or AIDS, a deadly, sexually transmitted disease that first appeared in white American gay men, would be attributed to black people whatever the evidence. Indeed, over the last five years US scientists, government officials and the media, aided and abetted by their counterparts in Western Europe, have been prodigious in their efforts to attribute the source of AIDS to black people, initially in Haiti and subsequently in the African continent, and to convey the message that the world AIDS pandemic is overwhelmingly an African problem.

If we can clear our minds of racist preconceptions and several years of 'AIDS from Africa' propaganda, it becomes strikingly clear that American and European scientists have not even wanted to look for a source of AIDS within the United States itself. As soon as the disease appeared in Haitians living in the USA, Haiti was immediately attributed, without evidence, as the source of the epidemic.

First the Haiti connection

Haiti is one of the poorest and most dependent countries in 'America's backyard', and the Haitian immigrants were amongst the most disadvantaged in the US. They were almost certainly misdiagnosed as suffering from AIDS when dying of wasting diseases, such as tuberculosis, that were associated with their poverty, and undoubtedly a number were surviving by prostituting themselves to wealthy Americans and were catching AIDS in the process. The truth emerged relatively quickly, and Haiti has now been largely forgotten.

For those who wished to propagate the belief that AIDS was not a US disease, Haiti was only a partial failure. Both the scientific community and the public at large showed that they were only too willing to believe that

the AIDS virus originated in black people somewhere. Where better, then, than 'darkest Africa'?

Next the African connection

The first Africans who developed AIDS were, in fact, Africans in Europe, many of whom had been resident there for many years. The idea that these people may have actually caught AIDS from Europeans and Americans never seemed to enter the minds of the doctors. And, like the Haitians, it seems probable that some of these early cases were not AIDS at all, as the number of new cases of AIDS diagnosed in Africans in Europe has in fact been declining between 1984 and 1986, and is only now showing a moderate increase.

In Britain the first recorded case in an African was that of a Ugandan woman who had been resident in the UK since 1963. When presented in **The Lancet** in 1984 the Ugandan connection was emphasised – she had been on a holiday to Uganda in 1979. At a recent international conference on AIDS and Africa in Naples, she did not appear on the list of African cases from the UK. We queried this with the Public Health Laboratories in Colindale, and were told she was now included amongst the British cases as she was resident in the UK. This juggling of African cases owes much more to politics and propaganda than to science.

Unreliable and unethical tests

Armed only with the belief that AIDS originated in Africa, teams of western doctors set off for Africa to find the source. They gathered together sick and dying patients and diagnosed them as suffering from AIDS to the exclusion of all other possibilities, and 'proved' that the AIDS epidemic in Central African cities was worse than in San Francisco and Los Angeles.

All their wildest speculations seemed confirmed when blood tests for AIDS became available in 1984/85. It is the blood tests that

Media coverage of the AIDS issue has been characterised by scapegoating, distortions and lies.

have been the basis of so much of the media speculation about the millions dying in Africa. Seroepidemiological studies have shown that anything between 10 and 50% of the population of sub-Saharan countries have been infected with the AIDS virus, although the number of AIDS cases in African countries has never been commensurate with this alleged incidence of virus infection. From the beginning there have been doubts about the validity of the commonly used blood tests, and a series of studies have shown that they are highly unreliable in those parts of the world, i.e. the tropical belt, where chronic malaria is common. In the West such studies have not been conducted because they are considered both unreliable and unethical.

Scientists initially considered AIDS to be an 'old disease of Africa', only spreading to the West with 'recent intercontinental travel', but they conveniently forgot the involuntary intercontinental travel of more than ten million Africans to the Americas, where they suffered frequent sexual abuse at the hands of the slave owners. Once these historical realities had penetrated the minds of the Western scientists, they came up with a new hypothesis that AIDS was a monkey virus that had recently crossed the species barrier in Africa and from there had spread to the rest of the world. They did not bother to explain why the disease first appeared in the US and from there spread to Western Europe, where the colonial ties between Africa and Europe would make a direct spread far more likely.

More bizarre theories

No explanation as to how the AIDS virus crossed the species barrier was too bizarre for consideration by the AIDS experts. African green monkeys were supposed to have been imported into Haitian brothels. According to two AIDS experts from St Mary's Hospital in London, Africans gave their children dead monkeys to play with as toys. A French doctor claimed that Africans injected themselves with fresh monkey blood as a sexual stimulant.

Although the West almost genocidally wants to believe that the epidemic in Africa is worse than in the rest of the world, the figures from the World Health Organisation have never supported this view. According to the latest figures (30th April 1988) there were 88,081 cases world wide, 65,464 in the American continent (57,575 of those were in the US), 10,851 in Europe (mostly Western Europe) and 10,639 from Africa.

African governments have been under intense pressure to produce sufficient bodies to satisfy the demands of the West, and their failure to do so has led to accusations that they are covering up to protect tourism. In reality some African governments have been over-reporting their cases. In the West, only cases of full-blown AIDS are reported to the World Health Organisation, but African governments have been encouraged to report patients who were merely seropositive.

Double standards

In the West three different positive blood tests for AIDS are required before the diagnosis is confirmed. In many African countries suffering under constraints imposed by the IMF, departments of health struggle to afford even the most basic and unreliable tests; and where no blood tests are available, they are encouraged to use clinical diagnostic criteria that do not distinguish between tuberculosis, African sleeping sickness and a range of other tropical diseases. These criteria will over-diagnose AIDS by approximately 50%.

But perhaps racism is not the only explanation for these attempts to blame Africa for the AIDS pandemic. US scientists, for example, isolated an Aids-like virus from Asian Macaque monkeys, but subsequently claimed to have isolated the virus in 'wild-caught' African green monkeys. When this work was challenged the scientists said there must have been a laboratory accident, a most unlikely story given the precautions taken to prevent contamination of laboratory staff with these deadly viruses. This was reported in the Guardian 8th March 1988 under the heading 'Africa not to blame yet'. You can be sure they are still trying. Is this sloppy science, or are we witnessing disinformation to cover up the true source of the virus?

Propaganda and political pressures

The US government has gone on the propaganda offensive over the issue of AIDS from Africa. African newspapers have been under pressure not to print articles suggesting an American laboratory origin, and US ambassadors throughout the world have countered suggestions that AIDS was a germ warfare experiment that went wrong with the scientific 'fact' that AIDS originated in Africa and had been there for thousands of years.

"There is mounting evidence that environmental pollution and the vast amounts of toxic substances we ingest in our food are related to a number of diseases which are on the increase and may be contributing to a deterioration of our immune systems. We must call a halt to genetic manipulations of animals and plants which have produced 'foods' devoid of vital nutrients, requiring large ammounts of toxic inputs, hormones, antibiotics and pesticides. AIDS may be only the first in a series of unusual and uncontrollable viruses."

Women's World, Isis 18 June, 1988

Well-funded organisations such as the Panos Institute, with large and well-equipped offices in London, Paris and Washington, have appeared suddenly, heavily promoting the 'AIDS from Africa' story. The Panos Institute claimed its specific role was to inform the non-governmental agencies in Third World countries and the media in the West about issues important in the Third

World, but its first, sensationalised dossier was all about AIDS and Africa.

As Third World governments are being progressively starved of funds, non-governmental agencies are playing an increasingly important role in the bureaucratic infrastructure in these countries. The Panos Institute's influence on the non-governmental agencies is unknown. Its influence on the media has been profound. Under the inevitable circumstances of economic dependency, doctors in Africa, under threat of economic sanction, are being pressured not to undertake AIDS research that would counter the idea of an African origin, but if they seek to promote the notion of AIDS as an African disease they are being rewarded with research grants and trips abroad.

The following acknowledgement has appeared at the end of several publications about AIDS in Zaire:

"We thank the Department of Health, Republic of Zaire, Mama Yemo Hospital, and the Ambassador Brandon Grove Jr, and the US Embassy, Kinshasa, for their cooperation and assistance."

It is not unusual to acknowledge organisations who have supported a research project, but this degree of direct political involvement by the US in research in a health matter in another country is quite remarkable.

Open Racism

The propagation of the idea that Africa is suffering the brunt of the AIDS problem has a reassuring effect on people in the West. On the other hand the consequences for Africa, and black people throughout the world, have been horrendous. All Africans are now treated as AIDS carriers, and are subjected to blood tests when seeking entry to many countries in Asia and Europe.

In Britain the Department of Health has advised doctors to consider all Africans and anyone who has been to Africa since 1977 or who has had sexual relations with an African as an AIDS risk. When a married British consultant at a London hospital died of AIDS

there was silence from the medical establishment and the newspapers were chastised for speculating about how he may have caught the disease. The DHSS even went to the extent of taking out court injunctions to stop newspapers reporting cases of AIDS amongst other British doctors. When a white married Zimbabwean doctor died of AIDS the response from the medical establishment was quite different. Although he had previously studied in Edinburgh where the incidence of AIDS is high, doctors went to the press claiming that he had caught AIDS in Zimbabwe, and the Health Authority where he had worked set up a hot line to reassure patients whom he had treated.

Fatal consequences

The AIDS problem in Africa is being emphasised to the detriment of the prevention and treatment of other diseases such as malaria that are major causes of morbidity and mortality, with the consequence that many more people may die of these diseases than actually die of AIDS. Indeed in Africa you are hardly allowed to die of anything else, and people with treatable diseases are no longer seeking treatment, in the belief that they are suffering from AIDS.

There are more sinister consequences of the widespread acceptance of the belief that AIDS is rampaging through Africa. There is no animal mode for AIDS infection, and trials of vaccine will require human volunteers. Western scientists are proposing that such trials should be conducted in Africa, and a controversial vaccine has already been used in Zaire with the approval of the Zairean ethical committee (in Mobutu's Zaire anything is possible). Are the people of Africa being 'softened-up' for the implementation of trials that would not be ethically acceptable in the West? There is a long history of this kind of exploitation of Third World countries, and as one African scientist pointed out, 'Once it proves useful its availability in Africa will immediately become scarce'.

THE POLITICS OF WOMEN'S HEALTH

What does *reproductive rights* mean?
"We want reproductive rights for all women, regardless of age, colour, class, disability, sexuality, or marital status. We may have very different experiences which may mean that we have different specific needs. But we all want the same thing – the right to information that will help us make our decisions, the right to adequate facilities, the right to decide on how we want to lead our lives as women. We realise this means a radical change in how women are seen in society. And we have to make demands in order for our voices to be heard and our needs recognised."
Women's Health and Reproductive Rights Information Centre, London

"We thought electronics was a clean industry. But it is the many chemicals and the radiation-emitting equipment we have to use that makes our work dangerous. Most of us workers are young unmarried women. We have discovered many of our illnesses – such as skin allergies, colds, headaches and eye problems – are work-related. A few of us also experience work-related problems which are special for women, such as irregular or difficult menstruation, urinary tract infections, and problem pregnancies... There is growing concern that that even our drinking-water may be contaminated by chemical leaks from nearby electronic plants. Some of these chemicals are known to cause birth defects and cancer."
The Plight of Asian Workers in Electronics Isis 3 1985

"People are paid to have sterilisations. The women are paid less than the men and the reason that is given is that a tubectomy is done at a greater expenditure to the government. She is not 'productive', but the man's work day is lost.. I have found that other contraceptive methods depend on what type of 'gifts' we are receiving as aid from governments or private agencies or voluntary agencies. One year we will get a supply of IUDs and all the programmes will be based on IUDs. The next year we will get condoms and all the programmes will be based on condoms. So if we get a lot of sterilisation kits meant for women, we will have tubectomies. There is no choice."
Ramala Buxamusa from the Women's University in Bombay, India, interviewed by the Concord Feminist Health Centre, USA

"This is what apartheid in health care and education means:
There are 28,318 white registered nurses and only 23,204 black nurses
although *the black population is six times greater than the white.*"
Anti-Apartheid Health Committee

"K.D.Matanzima, the 'president' of the Transkei Bantustan, described pregnancy as a 'self-inflicted disease'. Little wonder that no effort is made to improve the health of pregnant black women."
AAM Health Committee

"Birth control is the only free part of South Africa's health care system. In many rural areas, family planning is the only form of health care provided. Clearly there is an overwhelming preoccupation with preventing children being born, which is not mirrored by a concern about the health of those children who are alive already."
Anti-Apartheid Movement information

'useless pain'
Egyptian campaign against female circumcision
CFPA

Wendy Savage

Pam Isherwood / Format

BIRTH AND POWER

WENDY SAVAGE's suspension from medical practice in April 1985 for allegedly being a 'danger to her patients' provoked an enormous national furore. The unprecedented public enquiry (estimated to have cost the taxpayer at least £100,000) centred on only five of thousands of births for which she, as a consultant obstetrician, has been responsible. But the public, informed by the national and medical press, quickly saw the real issues at stake – those of medical power and practice. Her fight for justice and the principle of medical care that suits each individual earned her the loyalty of local women, patients and GPs, and the support of women and men everywhere. We print, with her kind permission, an extract from her disturbing and revealing book, _A Savage Enquiry: Who Controls Childbirth?_

33

Who controls childbirth?

The issue of birth and power is one which arouses strong emotions, because birth is a profoundly moving experience for all those who participate in the drama, whether as the person who should be the central point of the whole event, the woman, or the person who should be in a supporting role, the midwife or doctor. Birth arouses primitive and elemental feelings within us, reawakens unconscious or conscious memories in connection with our own beginnings and those of our siblings. It reminds us of death as well as life, the awareness of the tragedies which do still occur is not far from the surface.

Throughout history women have controlled birth in most cultures, and still do in many parts of the Third World. In the developed world men-midwives began to take over the control of birth in the eighteenth century. In the twentieth century the power of the obstetrician has risen to unprecedented heights. In the last forty years we have seen in this country a complete take-over of the whole process of birth by obstetricians, 88 per cent of whom are men at consultant level, where hospital policies are dictated. Only 1 per cent of women still have their babies at home, whereas before the Health Service almost half of all women delivered in their own homes. Midwives were responsible for the care of the majority of women and worked independently.

This major change in childbirth patterns in society has been followed by increased medicalisation of birth and rising rates of intervention, without good scientific evidence that these high rates are necessary. It is true that childbirth is safer than ever before, but the relationship between these improvements and many of the changes that have taken place in the 'management' of childbirth have not been properly evaluated and in particular, the fall in perinatal mortality is probably as much related to improved living standards and easier access to contraception and abortion as to neonatal intensive care and high technology in obstetrics – although for an individual woman these may make all the difference between a successful outcome and losing her baby.

Wendy Savage's supporters celebrate her victory in July 1986

Jenny Matthews / Format

In particular, antenatal care has not been subjected to rigorous analysis, and yet it has been accepted as essential to a good outcome. Fetal monitoring became widespread before its effectiveness was tested by a valid trial; induction of labour reached 40 per cent a decade ago, with no evidence that this high rate was necessary or even useful. And now the seemingly inexorable rise in the rate of delivery by Caesarean section is justified by some obstetricians for the sake of the baby, but although in some instances this is valid, in others the benefit is not proven.

Although obstetricians justify their takeover of birth by reference to improved outlook for mother and baby, and although there have been many advances for which women are grateful, there are still a large number of situations about which doctors lack adequate information to say which is the best course of action. My philosophy, in which I am not alone, of involving the woman in the decisions about her care, means the obstetrician must relinquish some power. Accepting that the woman should have control over her own fertility by means of access to contraception and abortion on her terms, not those of the medical profession, and understand-

ing that the woman should have choice about the way her pregnancy and labour is conducted, seems deeply worrying to some obstetricians – of both sexes. Such demands also challenge that power which has been based on a way of looking at evidence which proves the virtues of hospital or interventionist obstetric care over the traditional home-based, non-interventionist practice of midwives.

Although women may not have analysed their dissatisfaction with the care that they have received during childbirth, many hundreds have responded to my suspension by writing letters which show clearly that they do see this issue as

35

a struggle for the control of birth. Women – and the feminist movement – must involve themselves in this battle before we reach the situation in the USA where midwifery is illegal in most states, and where over 24% of women were delivered by Caesarean section in 1985.

What kind of services do women want and who is going to decide on the kind of care that is offered to them?

This is part of the wider issue about the way services are provided in the NHS: whether doctors and nurses are the best people to make decisions about what patients want, or whether administrators, either as non-practising doctors or as general managers with no medical background, should decide on grounds of efficiency alone. Sometimes when one looks at the cuts one feels that the ultimate hospital, as far as some planners are concerned, would be one which had no patients and thus required no revenue to run it!

My own feeling is that there needs to be a partnership between the consumers and the providers, both medical and administrative. It is too easy for professionals to become distant from the realities of patients' feelings. For example, doctors and midwives feel at home in hospitals, the surroundings are familiar, we know all the people, we have the pleasure and satisfaction of having accomplished worthwhile work in the building, and it is hard for us to see the place as an outsider does, frighteningly impersonal, overlarge, filled with people in a rush – and often associated with unhappy memories of illness or death. The routines, the forms, the technology may make some people feel secure but others feel lost and depersonalised – the very size overwhelms them. In this frame of mind understanding explanations becomes difficult, and the patient is acutely sensitive to attitudes and the way things are said and done.

There are two reasons why this debate is particularly contentious in obstetrics and gynaecology. Firstly, the majority of consultants are men, while the consumers are all women. Secondly, many of these women are not ill, they are seeking help and advice about how to avoid pregnancy, or how to get pregnant, how to obtain an abortion or what is best for themselves and the baby if they decide to embark on a pregnancy. Pregnancy is not an illness; it is a very important part of a couple's life together or a woman's life if she decides to go it alone. Women need help to achieve the kind of birth they want – about which many of them, even young women or those with little formal education, often have strong views. The role of a doctor is that of a counsellor rather than that of an authoritarian, trained professional, and this is very hard for some doctors to accept, especially the majority of male obstetricians.

The issue – of who decides on the type of care that a woman gets, the place that she delivers, the importance of her own views – has recurred over and over again in the letters that I have had from women. I think that obstetricians have to take a hard look at the way they are delivering services to women, and join with them in planning for the future so that the women have more say, and sterile confrontation is avoided.

The third issue is that of accountability

How is it possible that the Chairman of the Health Authority and a handful of doctors set in motion an enquiry costing an estimated £250,000 at a time when the impoverished district of Tower Hamlets is cutting beds and services? To whom is the Chairman of the District Health Authority accountable? To the people of Tower Hamlets? To the DHSS? To the North East Thames Regional Health Authority? To anyone? The Early Day Motion calling for his resignation was signed by over a hundred MPs in the fortnight between the publication of the first part of the report on 10 July and when Parliament rose on the 25th, but at the press conference on 24 July Francis Cumberlege seemed satisfied with his performance in this matter. He expressed no regret over the cost of the enquiry, nor the damage done to services.

To whom are the rest of the members of the DHA accountable? To the people of Tower Hamlets? To the bodies of whom they are nominees, but not representatives, i.e. the University of London, The Regional Health Authority, the London Borough of Tower Hamlets? The Local Medical Committee of GPs, the Medical Council of the London Hospital, or to none of these bodies? The whole system seems to lack any mechanism for assessing the performance of a Health Authority except in one way – can they keep within their budget?

To whom are hospital consultants accountable for the quality and organisation of their services? To the new General Managers? To the DHA? To the DHSS? To the GMC? To their patients or to no-one except themselves? As medicine is a self-regulating profession, in which, quite rightly, clinical autonomy is jealously guarded so that doctors have the right to decide what kind of treatment is best for an individual patient, to whom are doctors accountable – their professional colleagues as represented by the various Royal Colleges?

If the dissatisfaction with the way the maternity services are provided is to be overcome it is important that obstetricians, midwives and women meet together to discuss how best to use resources and what women want. Their conclusions must then be backed up by research. Midwives need to organise and regain their professional autonomy. Women need to be more involved in planning local services. Changes need to be made in the statutes relating to the appointment of consultants and the way that Health Authorities are formed to increase the representation of consumers. The medical profession needs to look at its institutions. We need to find a way to be more honest and less bureaucratic.

"I can say without hesitation that if the worse five of my own cases over a period of a year were put under a microscope, it would be possible to create a dossier similar to that of Mrs Savage. I believe the same could be done of every consultant obstetrician that I have ever worked with."

Peter Dunn, Reader in Child Health, Bristol University

GARBAGE MEANS BUSINESS

A recent OECD background paper states that traffic of toxic wastes from Europe to developing states 'could be very profitable and may well increase in the future'. Confirmed shipments of toxic wastes in 1988 from Europe to Africa include two loads of nuclear wastes from France dumped in Benin. The government of Benin reportedly took the wastes in exchange for economic aid.

One major exporter of wastes to Africa is Intercontrat SA of Fribourg, Switzerland. This firm joined by waste exporters in UK and US may ship up to 3.5 million metric tons of waste from N America and Europe to Guinea-Bissau. So far they have managed at least five shipments of toxic wastes from Italy to Koko, Nigeria, between March 1987 and March 1988.

In the 1980s the UK has become a major recipient of hazardous wastes from Europe, the US and New Zealand. The tonnage imported from Europe alone has increased from 5000 tons in 1983 to 25000 tons in 1985 to 250,000 tons in 1987, largely because British waste disposal fees are much lower than those in Europe.

Source: *International Trade in Toxic Wastes*, Greenpeace June 1988

DUMPING RADIOACTIVE FOOD

"..This House notes with anxiety reports that a consignment of dairy products was recently returned from Mexico to Ireland after the Mexican authorities claimed these were contaminated with radioactivity, notably Caesium 137, in all probability from fallout following the Chernobyl nuclear plant accident; further notes that similar claims for radioactive contamination of EEC dairy products have been made in Ghana, India, Brazil, Venezuela, Ethiopia, Somalia, Mozambique, Angola, Sri Lanka and Thailand.."

Source: *Notice of Motions*: Feb 1988, House of Commons Order Paper

LOW LEVEL LEAD

Four major studies, published recently, two from America, one from Australia and one from the UK, demonstrate highly significant relationships between foetal exposure to lead well within the normal range. and birth weight, head circumference and development during the first two years of life. The findings indicate that no child born into the modern world can be considered immune from the effects of low level lead exposure.

Source: *Clear* No 10 March 1988, the *Campaign for Lead Free Air*

ONE MOLECULE OF CHLORINE MAY WIPE OUT 100,000 MOLECULES OF OZONE

Already a hole the size of the USA has appeared in the ozone layer above Antarctica. An epidemic of skin cancers is likely to be the most immediately obvious effect. They estimate a 2.5% increase in CFCs (clorofluorocarbons used in aerosols and for making polystyrene hamburger cartons) could cause more than a million extra cancers, 20,000 of which would result in death.

The main producers of CFCs are multi-national companies like ICI, DuPont, Hoechst and Autochem. In the UK the only other company making CFCs apart from ICI is ISC Chemicals, a subsidiary of RTZ.

Source: *The Aerosol Connection*, 4th ed, Friends of the Earth

PESTICIDES

Last year (1986) over 26 million kilos of pure pesticides were used in the UK. Most are toxic to humans. Acute effects are nausea, giddiness, restricted breathing and even unconsciousness. In the short term they also act as irritants, affecting the skin, the lungs, the eyes or the gut. Chronic effects include cancers, tumour formation, birth defects, allergies, psychological disturbance and possible damage to the body's immune system.

The government and manufacturers say pesticides are safe and yet will not allow the public to see safety tests of those registered before 1986. Even if you want to see official 'evaluations' of pesticides tested after this date, it will depend on 'the Minister's discretion'.

Source: *Friends of the Earth Briefing Sheet*, Dec 1987

INCINERATION

The reason cities started building incinerators is because town dumps are filling up and polluting water supplies. Now they're dumping the same toxics that were in their garbage to start with, plus a whole new set created in the furnaces, except some are more concentrated and more soluble in water than they were in their original form.

What comes out of the stacks is just as frightening. Besides dioxins and furans, incinerators emit roughly 27 different metals, over 200 organic chemicals and a variety of acidic gases.The toxic effluent dioxin is actually created in the smokestack. The fatty tissues of citizens in several parts of the US contain average dioxin levels of 6.4 parts per trillion, a dosage sufficient to cause an 'unacceptable' increase in cancers in the exposed population. If all 220 proposed incinerators were built, dioxin emissions would bring the US population beyond the already 'unacceptable' level.

Source: Judy Christrup, *Rising from the Ashes*, Greenpeace vol 13 no 3 1988

BHOPAL encapsulates the economic and environmental implications of the pesticide industry. The plant was located in India by a US-based company, Union Carbide, to take advantage of the burgeoning developing world market in agrochemicals, and lax regulatory safeguards.

During a routine process of making Aldicarb, massive amounts of methylisocyanate were released, converting to hydrogen cyanide gas and killing more than 2000 people. Aldicarb is the pesticide implicated in one of the largest product recall emergencies ever, when Californian melons were found to be contaminated in the summer of 1985. It is also one the major pollutants found in Florida's ground water. Throughout its entire cycle, from production to contamination of food, soil and water, Aldicarb has proven to be a classic example of an uncontrollable chemical.

Source: John McCormick, *Diet for a Poisoned Planet*, Greenpeace vol 12 no 3 1987

One confirmed shipment of toxic wastes in 1988 from the USA was 15,000 tons of toxic ash from Philadelphia dumped on Kassa Island, Guinea. Guinea is trying to force Bulkhandling Inc. to re-export the ash.

Source: *International Trade in Toxic Wastes*, Greenpeace June 1988

Bikinians leave their island to make way for US atomic tests, 1946

USAF Defense Nuclear Agency

THE COSTS OF 'PEACE' IN THE PACIFIC

The first colonisers decimated vast indigenous populations with the common cold. Today, colonialism continues to have widespread and serious effects on the health of people all over the world. While the West has enjoyed a 'peace' based on nuclear deterrence, in the islands of the Pacific Ocean, the testing of nuclear weapons and the dumping of nuclear wastes have brought cancer, leukemia and malformed births to the people of the region. **LYNDA MEDWELL of the Nuclear Free and Independent Pacific Network shows how their health has also been devastated by displacement, cultural destruction, and denial of resources.**

In 1946, the United States detonated the first of a series of nuclear tests within Bikini Atoll in the **Marshall Islands**. The people of Bikini were given one month's notice, then moved 135 miles east to Rongerik Atoll. Here the well water was bitter, the fishing difficult and the coconut husks too inferior for making rope to build houses or to sell.

In 1947, a US Navy medical officer examined the Bikinians and found them *"visibly suffering from malnutrition"*. In 1948 the Bikinians were *"eating a variety of fish that was slightly poisonous ... and resulted in numbness of the arms and legs"*. The Bikinians were then moved to Kwajalein Atoll for medical care and feeding but were soon returned to Rongerik Atoll to resume a life where dependence on US supplies was clearly undermining their culture.

The Bravo Test

In 1954, the US exploded a 15 megaton hydrogen bomb called *Bravo* on Bikini. Atmospheric winds took the fallout over a number of inhabited atolls, including Rongelap and Utirik. Lijon Enkilang was seven years old in 1954, and lived on Rongelap:

"I woke with a bright light in my eyes. Soon we heard a loud noise, just like a big thunder, and the earth started to sway and sink. We were very afraid because we didn't know what it was ... two to three hours later we started to feel itching in our eyes ... Then came the fallout. It was white and to us kids we thought it was soap powder. The kids were playing in the powder and having fun."

Darlene Keju-Johnson is a health worker in the Marshall Islands:

"The people of Rongelap and Utirik were not picked up until three days after the explosion. Some American soldiers came and said, "Get ready. Jump in the ocean and get on the boat because we are leaving." People had to run fast. They were taken to Kwajalein. They didn't even give the people a change of clothing, so they slept in their contaminated clothes. You can imagine they were burnt and vomiting. Their hair was falling out, fingernails falling off, but they were never told why."

Rongelap

After their return to Rongelap five years later the Rongelap people experienced more and more thyroid problems and other illnesses. Convinced that these were due to contamination of their land and sea they reluctantly decided to leave their homeland to save the health of their children. But the US refused to resettle them. In 1985, the Greenpeace ship "Rainbow Warrior" moved the Rongelap people to an island called Mejato. They remain there today, dependent on outside aid, unable to pursue their traditional way of life – and coping with increasing incidence of illness. Darlene Keju-Johnson:

"The biggest problem ... especially among women and children, is cancers. We have cancers in the breast. We have tumour cancers. The women have cancers in their private places. Children are being born deformed ... We have this problem of what we call "jelly fish babies". They have no heads. They have no arms. They have no legs. They do not shape like human beings at all."

Currently the US is trying to wash its hands of compensation claims by giving a lump sum to the Marshall Islands Government. But this sum is inadequate to address the long-term consequences of the US testing programme.

In April 1988 Senator Jeton Anjain of Rongelap, testifying before a US Congressional hearing, requested $500,000 for a complete radiological study of Rongelap Atoll, to find out if the islanders could eventually return. He also

41

asked for assistance in finding an interim living place other than Mejato. In May, it was announced that both these requests had been turned down.

Ebeye

The people of Ebeye Island in Kwajalein Atoll have also suffered the pollution of their lagoon. Kwajalein Atoll is the primary US testing range for offensive and anti-ballistic missile systems including those involved in the "Star Wars" project. Until very recently, when public pressure finally had its effect, depleted uranium was used as ballast on the dummy warheads that crashed into the lagoon at 10,000 miles per hour often breaking up on impact.

Health problems of a somewhat different sort have also been created by the US presence. Three thousand Americans live and work on the 900 acre Kwajalein Island in conditions that are indistinguishable from many comfortable American suburbs. Three miles away on Ebeye, a tiny piece of coral, 8,500 people live crowded onto 66 acres in dilapidated housing amid appalling sanitary condition.

The US military has severely restricted access to the huge lagoon and to 93 islands traditionally used for fishing and agriculture. This has left the people of Ebeye totally dependent on wages on the base. But only 5–6% have jobs on the base, leaving the majority with little or no income. Darlene Keju-Johnson:

"The people of Ebeye have to survive on canned foods, rice and bread. We can't eat our traditional food – there is no space to grow breadfruit or coconuts. We have a problem with malnutrition. Children are not healthy because their diet is very poor."

Conditions on Ebeye have led to regular epidemics which are virtually impossible to control. In 1963 a severe polio epidemic left over 190 people paralysed at a time when polio vaccine had been available to Americans for nearly a decade. More recently, there has been an outbreak of tubercular meningitis and in 1988, two members of the US Navy on Kwajalein have been identified as AIDS sufferers. It is seen as only a matter of time before this latest imported disease takes its toll on the health of the Marshallese.

To cope with health problems on Ebeye there is one hospital, really a clinic, with only 12 beds. There is a large, fully-equipped hospital on Kwajalein – but only for US use. Residents of Ebeye have access to the hospital only on an emergency basis – and the US staff define "emergency".

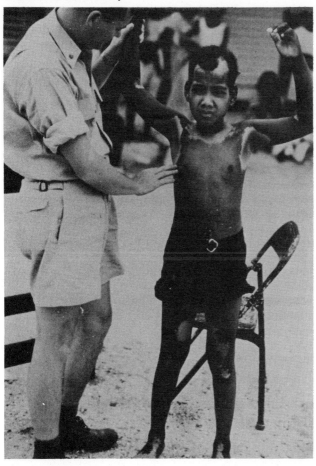

Iroji Kebenli of Rongelap suffered radiation burns from playing in "Bravo" fallout

The Marshallese Response

A report from the International Institute of Concern for Public Health recently stated:

Lack of access to adequate medical care and little or no health education are problems shared by every Marshallese outer island resident. These problems are acute. More infant deaths occur each month in the outer islands than the total deaths attributable to radiation effects over the last 30 years.

The Marshall Islands government is doing what it can to begin to remedy this situation.

A plan has been designed and is currently being implemented to develop an outer island dispensary system, called the Four Atolls Project. Health Assistants will reside in the communities and will deal with minor problems. A physician will visit each dispensary not less than six times a year. Any case requiring hospitalisation will be transported to Majuro Hospital.

French Polynesia

The French began nuclear testing in Algeria in the 1950's, then switched to Polynesia after Algerian independence. A French military spokesman explained that:

"The uninhabited atolls of Moruroa and Fangataufa were chosen for their distance from highly populated areas ... There are fewer than 48,000 people around Moruroa"

43

Before the French began the first series of tests in 1966, they announced a "Danger Zone" around Moruroa, in which people would not be allowed to travel until the tests were completed. When it was brought to their attention that seven inhabited atolls remained within the "Danger Zone", the French simply reduced the size of the zone until all the inhabited atolls lay outside it!

This was not the last instance of French manipulation of information. Prior to 1966, the French Polynesian authorities had routinely released annual statistics on causes of death in the territory. From the date of the first test, these statistics were no longer available.

Since July 1966, the French have released 41 bombs into the atmosphere in Polynesia, and have detonated 86 explosions underground. On Mangereva, babies experienced diarrhoea and sickness. Now more and more women are having malformed children and miscarriages and are suffering from cancer, thyroid conditions and leukemia. Yet the French government does not recognise that its tests have had any harmful effects at all.

The only medical data that has been produced by the French suggests that there was an average of 40 cancer cases per year in Polynesia between 1959 and 1965 compared with an average of 68 between 1977 and 1980. Fourteen cancer deaths were recorded between 1959 and 1962 compared with 40 between 1978 and 1982.

But these figure are inadequate and incomplete. They do not include people who go into private clinics, who see traditional healers or who go to France or elsewhere for treatment at their own expense. Nor do they include people on outlying islands who may never get to see a doctor at all.

The French government has prevented even its own National Radiation Laboratory from conducting studies in Polynesia and has resisted demands for an independent study. Recently the European Parliament Environment Committee has discussed sending an independent expert to Polynesia and a vote is likely in Strasbourg either in July or September. Meanwhile the French detonated their largest test for five years in May 1988 and there are more to come.

Fish Poisoning

Another illness connected with military and nuclear activities in Polynesia is a form of fish poisoning disease called ciguatera. The disease may last for five years and is sometimes fatal. Victims suffer severe muscular and nerve pain, diarrhoea and paradoxical sensations (hot water feels cold and vice-versa). The disease is caused by eating fish contaminated with the ciguatera micro-organism which spreads when coral reefs are ecologically disturbed.

On the island of Hao, no cases of ciguatera were recorded before 1965, when the French started construction of the nearby Moruroa military support facilities. In 1968, 48% of the people of Hoa had the disease. Other islands present similar statistics.

Apart from nuclear-related and other diseases, the people of Polynesia have suffered the destruction of their traditional culture and a massive influx of French settlers which has made them second-class citizens in their own land. Like the people of the Marshall Islands they remain confronted with long-term and widespread health problems whose origins are not of their own making, and whose solutions are beyond the scope of their efforts and resources.

Action and Support

Despite this the peoples of both the US Strategic Trust Territory in Micronesia and of French Polynesia have been active in combatting nuclear colonisation. There have been protests and demonstrations, sail-ins to restricted areas, laws suits in the US and French courts, testimonies at the UN, and before the French and US legislatures.

Protestors have sometimes paid the price: some of those struggling for a future for their people and their land have been imprisoned, injured and even killed. Neither the French nor the US seem ready to give up control over areas they regard as having military and strategic importance; but independence may be the only way for the peoples of the Pacific to escape continued exploitation. Please be active in support for the Pacific peoples.

PRIMARY HEALTH CARE

"Primary health care is generally lacking only when other rights are also being denied. Usually it is only lacking when the greed of someone goes unchecked and unrecognised (or unacknowledged) as being the cause. Once primary health is accepted as a human right, then the primary health worker becomes, first and foremost, a political figure, involved in the life of the community in its integrity. With a sensitivity to the community as a whole, he will be better able to diagnose and prescribe. Basically, though, he will bring about the health which is the birthright of the community by facing the more comprehensive problems of oppression and injustice, ignorance, apathy, and misguided good will."

Zafrullah Chowdhury of Gonoshasthaya Kendra, a community-based health programme in Bangladesh

UNHEALTHY OCCUPATION
an interview with Dr Jihad Mashel

DR. JIHAD MASHEL is a Palestinian doctor from the West Bank town of Ramallah. He works with the Union of Palestinian Medical Relief Committees (PMRC). While he was in Britain in May, Dr Jihad talked to Third World First about the health situation for the Palestinians under Israeli occupation in the West Bank and the Gaza Strip.

3W1: *Could you tell us about your work in the Occupied Territories?*

Dr J: I'm here as a member of the Union of Palestinian Medical Relief Committees, which is a non-political organisation in the West Bank and the Gaza Strip. The committees attempt to raise the standard of health in rural areas, and the consciousness of our people about health problems.

We started our work as a small group in Jerusalem in 1979, doing mobile clinics. These are teams of doctors, nurses and medical professionals, who go to villages and towns where there are no health services and try to help the people, by treating them and giving them health education. Through mobile clinics, we formed relationships with our people in rural areas, so that later we could establish permanent health centres. Unlike mobile clinics, permanent centres mean that you can follow up your patients, and deal with the causes of health problems in their village or region.

The object of our work is building the infrastructure for primary health care in the country.

So far we have eight committees in different regions of the country, such as the Gaza strip, Nablus and the Jordan Valley. In the mobile clinics, all the workers are volunteers. We have so far 700 voluntary members, 350 of whom are doctors. Only those who are working in the permanent medical centres are employed by the Union as full-time workers. Otherwise everything, including the administration and the organisation, is done on a voluntary basis.

We don't agree with charity, we are not a charitable kind of organisation, so we take a symbolic amount of money from each one we treat, except for the very poor people who we don't charge. We know which people are very poor, as the women and village health workers who work with us are themselves from the community.

3W1: *How are those village health workers trained?*

Dr J: The women selected undergo a nine month intensive training period in hospitals and outpatient clinics. This period includes both theo-

TERRITORIES OCCUPIED BY ISRAEL SINCE JUNE 1967

LEBANON
Quneitra
SYRIAN ARAB REPUBLIC
Nahariyya
Nawa
Haifa
Tiberias
Nazareth

MEDITERRANEAN SEA

Netanya
Jenin
Tulkarm
Nablus
Qalqiliya

Tel Aviv
WEST BANK

Ramle
Jericho
Amman

Jerusalem
Bethlehem

Gaza
Hebron
Dead Sea

GAZA
Rafah

Bersheeba

JORDAN

ISRAEL

EGYPT

SINAI

- - - - - Armistice Demarcation Line
- ·- ·- Boundary of Former Palestine Mandate
- ·· - International boundary

| 0 | 20 | 40km |
| 0 | 20 | 40mi |

The designations employed and the presentation of material on this map do not imply the expression of any opinion whatsoever on the part of the Secretariat of the United Nations concerning the legal status of any country, territory, city or area or of its authorities or concerning the delimitation of its frontiers or boundaries.

Elat

MAP NO. 3243 Rev. 1   UNITED NATIONS
SEPTEMBER 1985

The territory presently occupied and administered by Israel includes the Gaza Strip, the West Bank and the Syrian Golan Heights. The West Bank and Gaza are bounded by the armistice lines negotiated by the United Nation Acting Mediator in 1949; they were overrun in 1967.

retical and practical training. Later, they receive ongoing education, through lectures at the clinic. They may also attend short courses outside the village, or even outside the country if possible. Through this, they gain more skills and more experience.

This is the first time that village health workers in Palestine have been trained. They are women of 20 to 25, who are selected by their communities, and have completed the 10th grade at school, so they can read and write. Mostly they must be committed to the community, and have been active in it, through women's committees, and organising things like literacy classes and sewing classes.

3W1: *Do all these health workers in the villages tend to be women?*

Dr J: Yes, it was decided that they should be women for many reasons. Firstly, our communities are very conservative. Whereas a woman can get into any house and to talk with any person, a man cannot do so without permission. Also, most of our young women in the villages do not work, so they have time to give people. And thirdly, in primary health care there are many subjects to do with the relationship of the child and the woman, such as breast feeding, family planning and ante natal-care. In Arabic society, these are often unacceptable subjects for a man to teach.

3W1: *What are the living conditions like, for the people in the Occupied Territories?*

Dr J: About 50% of the people are living in rural areas, in villages. The Medical Relief Committees are working in the villages, as there are absolutely no other health facilities provided.

The rest of the people are in towns or in refugee camps. The camps were built as temporary measures, of breeze block that was designed to last 5 years. Often the houses crack or fall down. They are very close together. In Jabalia refugee camp in Gaza, there are 65,000 people. It is one of the most densely populated areas in the world and they are not allowed to build outside the area of the camp. The sewage system

in the camps consists of open canals, and these are a source of parasite infestation, especially among children. These canals cannot be closed for two reasons. Firstly, because the houses are built very close together, it is virtually impossible to plan and build a closed sewage system. What's more, if we build a closed sewage system, then we have to give up our refugee status, because the camps would then be considered permanent residences. This is an unacceptable solution. My family lives in a refugee camp, and we must live there until the Palestinian cause is resolved and we can go back to our homeland.

In the refugee camps, the health service is provided by the United Nations Relief and Works Agency (UNWRA), which was created specifically to support the Palestinian refugees, but this is not sufficient to take care of the great number of people who live there in overcrowded conditions.

3W1: *Why are these people living in refugee camps?*

Dr J: In 1948 part of Palestine had been occupied and the state of Israel had been declared there. All that remained was the West Bank and Gaza strip. The Green Line is the line that separates the West Bank and the Gaza Strip from the rest of Palestine. Over 700,000 arabs fled from the area inside the Green Line, and became refugees in the West Bank, the Gaza Strip, and surrounding countries, such as Lebanon. The refugee camps were set up at that time. Then, in 1967, Israel also occupied the West Bank and the Gaza Strip.

3W1: *Are there any Israelis living in the Occupied Territories?*

Dr J: Israel considers that the whole of Palestine is their promised land, so they have the right to build settlements anywhere in Palestine. They have settlements in the West Bank and the Gaza Strip. There are 120,000 settlers living in the West Bank and they are still building new settlements.

3W1: *Are the conditions for the settlers different?*

Louise Garner

**Dr. Jihad explains the connection
between open water channels
and parasitic infection
in El Ojer village**

Dr J: Yes. There are two categories of people, and two categories of health services. We are the oppressed people. We are not allowed to build without permission, we are not allowed to travel without permission, not allowed to own land without permission. The Israeli settlers claim it is Israeli land – the promised land of God. They can travel whenever they wish. We have special identity cards to identify who is Palestinian and who is Jewish. Many restrictions exist in order to keep us oppressed. They limit our ability to do work, to travel around, and to develop our own infrastructure. These restrictions apply to all sections of life.

One issue which highlights our position is the water restriction. A few hundred Israeli settlers may have a swimming pool, yet the Palestinian village next door has to have rationed water. Water is only available on a meter for a few hours every day and you need a license to dig a well.

From the very beginning, land with water was taken for their settlements. They confiscated it and they took the water resources – springs and everything. They wanted to have it under their control. It is not permitted for us to dig a well for irrigation, but for any Israeli settler it is a simple matter.

Some of our villagers drink from polluted water running through open canals. This has been a problem for hundreds of years. But now we cannot solve this problem by having a system of closed pipes, as permission to build them has been refused. Yet Israeli settlers in the same are have water, from the same spring, running through closed pipes. When you are talking about health and sanitation, water is absolutely necessary, and is a political issue.

49

3W1: *Of course, to help people's health and to enable the poorest people, in any way at all, is an intensely political activity, isn't it?*

Dr J: We cannot say that it is not political. The Israeli authorities are trying to destroy the infrastructure of the people. They want to stop us organising. We cannot register our clinics under the organisations name, because of restrictions. All the permanent clinics are registered under private names, so they cannot close them legally. There are restrictions on all grass roots organisations. We are trying to raise the health conditions that exist. But our work is humanitarian, we don't have a political policy. Everyone has the right to have his own opinion about what might happen and how things should be done. The only policy we all agree on, is to help poor people in our rural areas and build primary health care. But in our country breathing is a political issue.

3W1: *What are the major health problems that have to be faced?*

Dr J: Malnutrition is one of the most prominent problems. 34% of people in the Jordan valley and up to 40% of the population in some villages are affected. Secondly, anaemia affects 20% of the people, mainly women and children. Thirdly, parasite infestation is common in villages because of the water pollution and in refugee camps because of the sewage system and the overcrowding. It affects about 40–60% of the people. And now, since the uprising started, we face additional problems. We have had to intensify our work to treat not only those injured by shooting or tear gas or beatings, but also people unable to go to doctors and unable to get their medication. Some of them suffer from chronic diseases such as hypertension or diabetes mellitus which need constant medication. During sieges and restrictions most of these people could not get medication so complications had set in. So they have been indirectly injured by the situation.

Among those injured, hundreds will not go to government hospitals because they must be reported to the security forces and may be arrested for being in demonstrations. People who **50**

may be badly injured or have complications may seek traditional medicine at their homes, but often this is ineffective.

3W1: *So there are many new difficulties, because of the Israeli action in the last months... How are the Medical Relief Committees coping with these?*

Dr J: At the moment we are responding to three major difficulties. We are training our people in First Aid, because at the moment there are many injuries, and lots of places do not have services at all. We have given hundreds of lectures in different places. We distribute leaflets in simple arabic and plastic bags containing first aid material, which may help to save a life, to stop bleeding, to fix a hand or a leg. We distributed thousands of such kits, but we need to distribute them to all our people.

Also, the blood banks cannot cope with the amount of blood needed, so we have to get donations quickly. Therefore, we are running a campaign for testing blood groups so everyone can carry a card stating their group, in case they need to give or receive blood. Often, getting donations is difficult anyway, because of the curfews. For example, on Land Day in March, everywhere was under curfew. When four people from one family in Ramallah were injured, two of them died because they could not get blood transfusions.

Every day we have to supply our people with medications and drugs. So far we have examined 25,000 people. And we are going to have to treat many more thousands of people because we are still under siege, under curfew, the beating policy is still in force, there are planned attacks. We have to be ready to deal with these situations, at any time. So, in particular, we need medications, and for this we need support through institutions and donations.

3W1: *So what is your purpose in Britain? What can we do here?*

Dr J: I hope to keep the kind of concern shown at the beginning of the uprising by the people, the medical professionals and organisations in

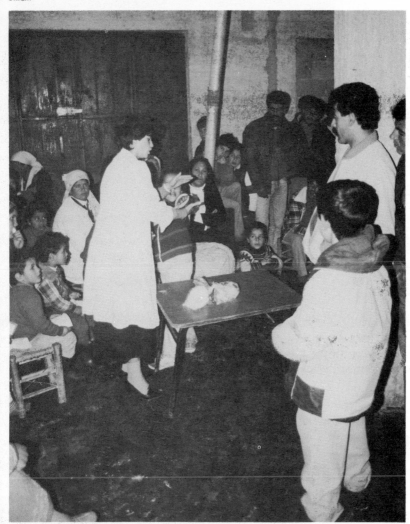

An MRC Doctor talks on First Aid in a West Bank village

Britain, alive. We hope that pressure will be put on the Israeli authorities so they do not continue with their policy. Also, we hope to gain the solidarity for our people in different places. People must support them materially and spiritually in their fight against occupation. I want to inform people that what was happening in February in Palestine, is still happening and never stopped.

(For more information on the situation in Palestine, see 'Palestine: Education Under Siege' in Links 31: *Students and Struggle for Change*)

War is bad for the health. More than 500 people were killed when Ethiopian MiGs bombed this Eritrean village

"THERE HAS TO BE COMMUNITY PARTICIPATION!"

Primary health care in Eritrea

The Eritrean People's Liberation Front are fighting drought and famine as well as a repressive regime. They regard the health of the people as an end in itself but also crucial to the success of their long struggle. Third World First spoke to the coordinator of their Public Health programme, DR. NERAYO TEKLE MICHAEL.

Dr N: In Eritrea we have been trying to establish a primary health care scheme. Conditions have been immensely unfavourable – a drought and famine for ten years and a war of liberation for 25 years – but to a large extent we have been successful. There are basic requirements for the proper implementation of primary health care and we think we have some of the answers.

3W1: *What are those answers?*

Dr N: There has to be community participation. This has wide implications, in that, if people make decisions about their health they might also decide about their economy, their security and their education, women's rights and so on. If they are encouraged to come together, they can also solve their problems together. Our task has been mainly to act as a catalyst and that is the most important lesson we could have learnt.

3W1: *How does war affect the health of people in Eritrea?*

Dr N: The war has had a tremendous effect upon the health of the people. This is felt directly through war injuries and bullet wounds, but indirectly as well. If there has been a heavy air-raid the incidence of miscarriages in pregnant women may rise. Therefore the war not only leaves physical scars but also mental ones which ultimately effect the health and the quality of life of the people. They become insecure because they are driven away from their homes and have to cross borders to escape the war. The stability of life is disrupted. Shortage of food and diseases such as malaria are added problems.

3W1: *Can you describe the primary health care programme and how it has been adapted to the situation in Eritrea?*

Dr N: The first step for a successful primary health care scheme is that it should be accessible to everyone. So it should be as near as possible to the settlements and villages. It is too expensive to have a large health centre for every village – there simply are not the trained staff available at the moment.

For every village of 500–1,500 people we have two people based in the village who are trained. They are the village health worker and the traditional birth attendant. As part of the community, they see and know everybody in the village. They are responsible to the village council, which is responsible for their selection and the role of the government is limited to providing formal training, supervision and moral support.

3W1: *What happens at the regional level?*

Dr N: In the sub-districts there are health stations which cover about 10 villages and then there are regional hospitals and one health centre. For a district of 50,000 people there is a health centre which is run by about 50 people. In the whole of Eritrea we have 300 health stations and maybe 50 health centres and six regional hospitals.

The place of training should be as near as possible to the place where people will actually be working. The training for paramedical workers does not take long. The doctors have a more academic training, over a longer period – a year to 18 months. At the health centre level, we try to cover most of the specialities so that people do not need to travel a long distance to receive medical treatment. We have learnt from experience that if a hospital or a clinic is further than 15 km, people tend not to bother to go.

In some health centres we have a mobile unit which provides health care for the nomadic population – something like 25% of the population. We have clinics along their routes and when they stay somewhere (which is for about 2–3 months) we can provide health care for them. In the past people have criticised the way of life of the nomads, but we feel that they have a way of life which should be respected. We have to try to improve their quality of life. The thing which they lack is good health – especially for women who are pregnant. If their health is improved then the children they bear will be healthy.

3W1: *Which particular issues of women's health have been addressed?*

Dr N: The most important thing is nutrition, especially during the periods of pregnancy and breast feeding. We are trying to change the eating habits of the family, because the man gets his food first, leaving the leftovers to the rest of the family. The family should eat as a unit and share the food on an equal basis. Then the nutrition of women will improve.

There are lots of problems about women's circumcision. The EPLF's (Eritrean Peoples Liberation Front) public health organisation condemns women's circumcision and this old tradition is slowly changing.

3W1: *What is happening with the production of sanitary towels?*

Dr N: Providing women with a free supply of sanitary towels where before it was a matter of making their own, is revolutionary in terms of the relative freedom it gives. It is important for the urbanised women who have used them before and who are now living in the liberated areas of the countryside, though it would be difficult to provide sanitary towels for every woman in Eritrea. Of course, women have their own methods. They have a kind of circular wooden seat which they sit on, over absorbent sand. Others wash themselves with sand. In some areas women have tried to use cloths as sanitary towels but, because women do not wear underwear as they do in the West, it is difficult to hold the cloths in place. The machine for producing the sanitary towels was bought by the Union of Eritrean Women in exile, who continue to provide the raw materials. The towels are distrib-

uted throughout the liberated areas. The Department of Hygiene which is responsible for this factory is also developing local soap production.

3W1: *What is happening in the area of drug production?*

Dr N: There are several thousand types of drugs available in the world but we have our own list of about 200 essential drugs. We save vast amounts of money if we produce our own drugs and we see this as a fundamental project.

Drugs occupy nearly 60% of expenditure on health care and there may be delay or failure in supply. It takes about 8 months to get drugs from the stage of ordering until they arrive. Prices are high and transport expensive, so it makes sense to produce our own medical supplies. Drug production has not solely concentrated on modern medicines and we produce traditional medicines from local sources.

3W1: *What developments have there been in artificial limb manufacturing?*

Dr N: As a result of the war there is an ever-increasing number of amputees and the production of artificial limbs has been going on for some time.

We do have a problem with supplies and have found that the best way is to use local materials. At the centre we have nurses and people who have been trained locally. Many people have been fitted with artificial limbs especially those with amputations below the knee. Above the knee it is a little bit more difficult because then it requires quite a lot of wood and because of this the limb is very heavy. In these instances it would be better to use synthetic materials which are light and strong but these are not cheap. The prosthesis workshop is an extremely important addition to our facilities.

3W1: *What sort of health education takes place?*

Dr N: We teach people about the problems around them. Of course the prevailing problems are bad sanitation, hygiene and nutrition. The

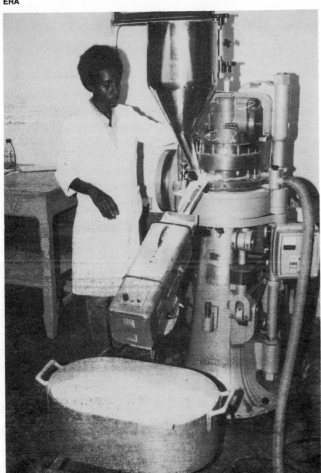

This tablet press machine is part of the Eritrean generic drug manufacturing programme

availability of water is crucial. Without water, it is difficult to establish any kind of successful sanitation system to maintain standards of hygiene.

The most important issue is adequate nutrition for the people. Some ask why it is an issue, when we have so little food anyway. Firstly, if people are taught about nutrition then they will be able to produce more of the right foods – those which are important to them. If they have more of the right food then they will be able to produce more because they are more healthy, and so eventually it will change people's lives radically.

Secondly, if we teach them about nutrition it will enable them to use the little amount of food they have in the right way. With repeated health education, people can increase their production of food. That is why health education is essential.

THE PEOPLE'S VOICE!
A conversation with a Tigrayan health worker

After the 1975 Tigrayan revolution, the Tigray People's Liberation Front (TPLF) aimed to make primary health care available to the whole population in as short a time as possible. Despite the harrassments of war, four hospitals and a network of clinics now serve the four million or so people in the liberated area. Hundreds of people from peasant communities have been trained at the Central Hospital as 'physicians' (dressers), pharmacists, laboratory technicians, midwives and community health workers. They are trained in diagnostic and treatment techniques for the common epidemic diseases and ailments and in preventive health education and action.

At the remote village of Awhie, physician GEBRE LIVANOS described to Third World First how he came to Awhie and his work at the clinic.

Jenny Hammond / 3W1

Gebre Livanos outside the clinic at Awhie

My name is Gebre Livanos and I am the second physician here. The senior physician is a away at a seminar. I was elected from the peasants in 1982. Until people elect a trainee, fighters are assigned as physicians. I have my wife and children with me. Two of my children died of famine, both girls, aged three years and one year. Another daughter drowned when she was fourteen in the flood in the river. Now I have two boys of sixteen and eight and a girl of ten.

This area is a resettlement area and when people began coming here in 1982, this clinic was built to serve them. This community came from two different *woreda* (districts) in the highlands. At first there were problems, but eventually they were sorted out by marriage. We are one *tabia* (scattered farms making a village) of about 137 households. An average of forty to fifty people a day are treated here. The numbers go up in September and October, when malaria is at its peak, and decrease from November. Yesterday (28th January), I treated eight patients with malaria, three with anthrax and five with simple injuries.

The main health problems are epidemic diseases. The most widespread is malaria, but because we can control it, it is not the worst. TB is a greater problem because of shortage of medicines. We have TB of the neck, of the genital organs and of the lungs. There are only a few cases but we are not in control like malaria. Two TB patients have recently been referred to the bigger clinic at Edaga Hibret. They are still under treatment there.

Young children are always at risk, but since the revolution clinics have been set up everywhere and child mortality is decreasing all the time. When they get malaria we can control it with drugs. The problems come, not at birth or with newborns, but at one or two years, especially with chicken pox. Eight babies under a year old have recently died of chicken pox. One of the difficulties is that the families keep them at home. They don't want to bring them to the clinic because of the superstition that it is a punishment from god. But we are working against this and the understanding of the people is improving.

The most important aspect of health care is preventive health education, especially personal sanitation and environmental hygiene. The building of latrines comes first, then burning or burying rubbish. We use isolation to prevent epidemics spreading. People are following this advice and most households now have their own latrines. We encourage people to come *early* to the clinic when they are ill and we now have trained health workers serving up to ten houses who are responsible for monitoring conditions.

One of the worst diseases we have to deal with is anthrax. It starts with an infected spot and it kills if is not treated within seven days. It is not new for us and is not restricted to the lowlands; it is in the highlands too. The infection is caught through contact with faeces, especially by people who share their houses with their animals. Since the preventive health programme has encouraged the building of animal houses outside the village which are regularly cleaned, we have begun to see improvements.

Awhie is in the lowlands, where there is plenty of land, but also plenty of mosquitoes. The people have come here from the central highlands in search of land. Above 2000 metres there is no malaria but there is also very little land. But even there people have to come down sometimes to the valleys for water or journeying to markets, and then they catch malaria.

I too have come from the central highlands. Under Haile Selassie I worked in a private pharmacy, then I went to Humera where a large mechanised farm had been set up. I worked there with other physicians. Then I returned to the central highlands because I got married and thought it would be better to stay in my homeland. All this was before the overthrow of Haile Selassie in 1974.

After the revolution in Tigray (1975), when I was living in the liberated area, there was famine in my area and shortage of land, so I wanted to resettle my family in Western Tigray. I wanted land. But TPLF fighters came to know my skill and wanted me to become a public physician, so they refused my request to let me move. But when a new fighter came who didn't

Dr. Samual Zemarian talks to young patients at the Western Region hospital in Tigray

two or three times. As there was no health education for the people, many of the problems were unnecessary and preventable and many were dying of epidemic diseases.

When I came here I went for training in Adi Mehameday for six months. In the central highlands I was also a veterinarian and for a while after coming here also. But now the TPLF have organised training for veterinarians and, since five vets from this area have been elected from the people, I don't give veterinary advice any more.

Before all, I want to tell you my own personal story. You see, before I went to the training centre, most of the time I didn't want to be a physician. I only

know me, I persuaded him to let me register for resettlement and so I came here. Then after I arrived, the fighters here also encouraged me to become a physician, so I agreed.

Before that I was not trained properly at all. In the time of Haile Selassie, in Asmara and Humera, physicians like myself were not trained, so I was very hesitant about giving treatment and diagnosing diseases. All clinics used to be private – even in the towns there were few clinics and in the countryside there was nothing. The peasantry and poor people in towns had no chance of health care. We would treat the serious cases as well as the simple cases. We never sterilised syringes and we'd use them for

wanted to be ploughing my own land. It seemed a much better way to feed my family. But now I understand that I am in a better way of life to be a physician and help the people.

Now I am very proud. Really, for a poor peasant to be a physician and help the people ... it is a wonderful thing. All the peasants who live here really appreciate our organisation (the TPLF) because of this clinic. You see, before, no peasant had a chance to have treatment near his house and would have to travel many kilometres. Now we have a clinic in our own village and we are proud and feel glad and happy to be treated here.

BRING ON THE HEALTH BRIGADISTAS!

The new revolutionaries in Nicaragua are the health workers and teachers. Because they are at the forefront of social transformation, they are also in the front-line of the war and have become a special target of Contra raids. The NICARAGUA HEALTH FUND gives us the latest news of the situation.

Nicaragua Health Fund

Literacy classes play a crucial part in the struggle for improved health in Nicaragua

In Nicaragua, health is seen as the responsibility of organised people's groups. 'People's health councils' enable trade unions, neighbourhood organisations, and associations of young people and women to take an active role in carrying out health programmes. Co-ordinated by the people's health councils, the 'health-days' have become the leading edge of campaigns against malaria, dengue fever, polio and measles. In 1981, the malaria and dengue campaigns involved 1.9 million people (70% of the population).

Health in Nicaragua has been a human right since the revolution in 1979. Nicaragua's health and social security systems were reorganised to begin building a comprehensive primary health care system. In four years, the number of health posts and health centres was trebled, and over 80% of the population had access to free primary health care.

Contra Attacks on the Health Care System

But many of the dramatic accomplishments which led the World Health Organisation to recognise Nicaragua in 1982 as the developing nation that had made the greatest progress in health care have been undercut by the impact of the war.

Such attacks are part of a broader strategy disarmingly termed 'low-intensity conflict' (LIC) by U.S. Officials. LIC is an outgrowth of counter-insurgency operations in Vietnam. Today, this strategy is being applied in countries such as Ethiopia, Afghanistan, Angola, Lebanon, the Philippines and Nicaragua. LIC relies upon covert actions, military operations by surrogates, disinformation and economic destabili-

On March 7, 1987 37 year old Ambrosio Gonzalez, was abducted by several armed men who came at night to his home asking for him by name. When his family dared venture out of the house, they found him nearby, badly beaten and his throat slit. His death left eight children and a pregnant widow.

On March 29, 1987, Maria Pinera, 24, was kidnapped by armed men from her mother's house near Waslala, where she lived with her three small children. She has not been heard from since.

The common bond that led to Ambrosio's death and Maria's disappearance was their profession. He was a health volunteer. She was a nursing assistant. They are two of more than 100 health workers who have become casualties in the war in Nicaragua, all of them victims of the USA-CIA financed military forces known as contras. The contras' major objective is to overthrow the government of Nicaragua.

Nicaragua Health Fund papers

"...we couldn't approach one village because there are people in the area that consider this type of work – building latrines and clean water systems – a "communist" activity and it would put the participants in personal danger".

" In the war zone, 20 per cent of the health centres functioning in 1983 were either destroyed, attacked or closed due to threats by contras. The contras would then demand to know the identity of those in the village engaged in health, teaching, local government or agricultural co-operatives. These individuals would then be kidnapped or executed".

Testimony of Nicaragua Health Workers
Nicaragua Health Fund papers

An article published on 13 February, 1987 in the *American Medical Association News* said: *"We found the contra forces were implicated in all six of the attacks (on the health clinics) we studied. In five of the six instances, there was no military target located nearby that could account for the heavy fire against the medical installations."*

sation to achieve political objectives. In contrast to conventional warfare, LIC targets civilian populations. LIC makes 'rational' the seemingly irrational contra policy of targeting not only health centres, but also schools, the agricultural sector and international technicians.

There is little doubt that such attacks are part of a deliberate strategy to destroy the health care system, including public health campaigns, in the countryside. As a result of the deaths of French and German doctors, a Swiss medical technician, and a Spanish nurse, most foreign volunteers had to be withdrawn from the war

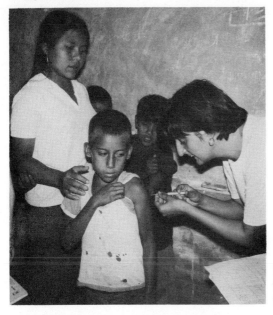

**Health workers are in the
front line in the war against
the Contras**

zones. It is estimated that the health care system has sustained more than $30 million in damages, resulting in the loss of health services for up to 15% of the population.

Between 1983 and 1985, the number of visits to physicians fell by 15%, and visits by infants and children under the age of four fell by 37%. Numbers of malnourished children participating in supplementary feeding programmes fell by 10% and post-partum care of low birthweight babies fell by 19% in the same period. Mass vaccination and malaria control programmes have been significantly disrupted in the countryside. After 1984, vaccination coverage for measles declined in some war zones with other communities remaining wholly unvaccinated. During a 1986 vaccination programme, ten health workers were killed when a mine destroyed the vehicle in which they were travelling.

A recent study found that in the provinces most heavily affected by the war, there was a 17% increase in reported malaria cases between 1983 and 1985, while in the less affected provinces, there was a 62% reduction. One of the war zones is reported to have a ten-fold increase in

tuberculosis and resistant strains are more prevalent due to incomplete courses of treatment.

In the first four years after the revolution, education and health care accounted for 50% of the national budget. Only 18% was allocated to defence. Those figures are now reversed and as a consequence, many development programmes have been suspended. Some US supply and shipping companies have refused to sell or ship medical materials to Nicaragua. The resulting impact of the embargo on Nicaragua's hospital has been severe, and has led one administrator to refer to his institution as a *"cemetery of broken equipment"*.

The psychological consequence for the civil population will no doubt be among the most serious and long lasting health effects of the conflict. The aggravation of daily life due to the war, have all exacerbated anxiety and depression, family and community strife, as evidenced by the significant increases in the demand for outpatient psychiatric services. Many of the 9,000 children orphaned by the war are at considerable psychological risk.

RESOURCES

ORGANISATIONS

Afro-Caribbean Mental Health Association
35-37 Electric Avenue, London SW9 8JP 01 737 3603

Black Communities Aids Team (BCAT)
Landmark, 47 Tulse Hill, London SW2 2TN 01 671 7611

Black Health Workers and Patients Group
259a High Road, London N15 01 809 0774

Black Lesbian and Gay Centre
Unit 4, 2 Somerset Road, London N17 9QP 01 885 3543

The Black Unity Group
The Worland Centre, 10 Vicarage Lane, London E15 01 555 1122

Council for the Advancement of Arab-British Understanding (CAABU)
21 Collingham Road, London SW5 ONU 01 373 8414

Disability Alliance
25 Denmark Street, London W2 7ND 01 289 1601

Eritrean Relief Association (ERA)
391 City Road, London EC1V 1NE 01 837 9236

Foundation for Women's Health Research and Development (FORWARD)
Africa Centre, 38 King St, London WC2 8JT 01 379 6889

Friends of the Earth Trust Ltd
26-28 Underwood Street, London N1 7JQ 01 490 1555

Greenpeace International
25-26 High Street, Lewes, East Sussex BN7 2LU 0273 478787

Health Action International (HAI)
Emmastraat 9, NL-2595 EG, The Hague, Netherlands

Health Resources and Technologies Action Group (AHRTAG)
1 London Bridge Street, London SE1 9SG 01 378 1403

Health Rights
344 South Lambeth Road, London SW8 1UQ 01 720 9811

Nafsiyat Inter-Cultural Therapy Centre for Ethnic and Cultural Minorities
278 Seven Sisters Road, London N4 2HY 01 263 4130

International Institute of Concern for Public Health
67 Mowat Avenue, Suite 343, Toronto, Ontario M6K 3E3 Canada

Irish in Britain Representation Group Camden Branch
12 Greenland Street, London NW1 0LU 01 482 0869/0824

London Hazards Centre
3rd Floor, Headland House, 308 Gray's Inn Road, London WC1X 8DS
01 837 5605

London Irish Women's Centre
59 Stoke Newington Church Street, London N16 01 249 7318

National Abortion Campaign (NAC)
Wesley House, 4 Wild Court, London WC2B 5AU 01 405 4801

Nicaragua Health Fund
83 Margaret Street, London W1N 7HB 01 580 4292

Organisation for Lesbian and Gay Action (OLGA)
PO Box 147, London SE15 3SA 01 833 3860

Palestine Solidarity Campaign
BM PSA London WC1N 3XX

Rational Health Campaign
Oxfam House, 274 Banbury Road, Oxford OX2 7DZ 0865 56777

Relief Society of Tigray (REST)
27 Beresford Rd, London N5 2HS 01 359 9406

Teaching Aids at Low Cost (TALC) Primary Health Care Resources
PO Box 49, St Albans, Herts AL1 4AX 0727 53869

Terence Higgins Trust Ltd
Helpline, BM A.I.D.S. London WC1 3XX 01 833 2971

Tigray Solidarity Campaign
PO Box 528, London SW9 9DD

Union of Palestinian Medical Relief Committees
c/o CAABU or PO Box 19369, Jerusalem

Women's Health and Reproductive Rights Information Centre
52-54 Featherstone Street, London EC1 01 251 6332

Women working for a Nuclear Free and Independent Pacific
c/o Lynda Medwell, Birchwood Hall, Storridge, Malvern, Worcs WR13 5EZ

PUBLICATIONS

A Savage Enquiry: Who Controls Childbirth? Wendy Savage, Virago 1986

Across the Water M Lennon M McAdam & J O'Brien, Virago 1988

Adverse Effects: Women and the Pharmaceutical Industry Kathleen McDonnell, Health Action International

Aids, Africa and Racism Richard Chirimuuta, The Author 1987

Aids and Sexual Politics Simon Watney, 1987

Aids and the New Puritanism Denis Altman, Pluto 1986

Bitter Pills: Medicines and the Third World Dianna Melrose, OXFAM 1982

Cleared for Export Andrew Chetley, Coalition against Dangerous Exports (CADE) 1985

Drug Pushers THIS London E2 01 739 9093

Helping Health Workers Learn David Werner, TALC

Hoechst – A cause of Illness? BUKO Pharma-Campaign Germany 1987

Northern Ireland: The Political Economy of Conflict B Rownthorne & N Wayne, Polity Press 1988

Our Bodies Ourselves: A Health Book by and for Women Boston Women's Health Collective; Brit.eds. Angela Phillips Jill Rakusen Penguin 1978

Oxford Medical Publications OUP Oxford OX2 6DP 0865 56767

Primary Health Care in Eritrea J Black & Y Fassil, ERA 1986

Radical Community Medicine (Quarterly) London N19 01 281 0922

Towards Rational Drug Use Health Action International (HAI) 1988

Where There Is No Doctor David Werner, TALC

Women's Health A Spare Rib Reader Sue O'Sullivan, Pandora

VIDEOS

Hard to Swallow OXFAM 274 Banbury Road, Oxford OX2 7DZ 0865 56777

Nightmare in Paradise Concord Films Council Ltd
201 Felixstowe Road, Ipswich, Suffolk IP3 9BJ 0473 76012

When Breasts are Bad for Business Baby Milk Action Coalition
34 Blinco Grove, Cambridge CB1 4TS 0223 210094

LINKS PUBLICATIONS

Other Links publications containing articles on health issues:

17 Women's Work, Women's Lives

19 Reclaiming the Earth

23 The Colonial Carve-Up

24 Transnational Corporations: Real International Terrorists?

26 Critical Mess: The Real Costs of Global Nuclearisation

27 Knowing Women: Women and Educational Alternatives Worldwide

29/30 Singing Our Own Songs: A basic guide to underdevelopment and struggle for change

Links 34   Images of Third World People
The dominant view of 'Third World' people is as victims of crises such as famine, or in stereotypes which emphasise the 'savage' or the exotic. Development agencies, as commentators on development issues, play a key role in shaping public perceptions of the Third World. This Links investigates, first, the extent to which development agencies and large-scale media events such as Band Aid have reinforced dominant perceptions; second, how the agencies have responded to the issues of politics, racism and equal opportunites within their development education policies; thirdly, how Black cultural workers are reclaiming images of themselves to present an alternative image of Black struggles in Britain and the Third World.
Published January 1989

Links 35/36   Women in the Revolution in Tigray
Under the centuries-old feudal system, women in Tigray were severely oppressed and exploited. The average age of marriage was nine years; women could not own land; yet they were expected to perform hard labour on the land as well as all domestic tasks; they were subject to routine violence; they had no rights, legal or domestic, and no voice in private or in public affairs; genital mutilation was the norm. After the 1975 revolution, however, women were declared 'half the revolution'. They have been given equal rights before the law, equal access to land, a voice in the administration of their communities. The lowest legal age of marriage has been raised to fifteen. Using the testimony of the women themselves and her own experiences inside Tigray, Jenny Hammond investigates this transformation of life for Tigrayan women and looks at the difficulties they face not only from their traditional culture but from the ravages of constant war.